Soul Salvation

I JUST DON'T GET IT?

RUMIKA E. MCKNIGHT

All Scriptures used are from the King James Version (KJV), New King James Version (NKJV), English Standard Version (ESV), New Living Translation (NLT), and New International Version (NIV).

Cover design and layout by: Rumika E. Mcknight
Book formatted and finalized by:
Kingdom Promise Publishing LLC
Kingdompromisepublishing.com
FB: @kppublishingllc

ISBN: 978-1-7373357-0-2
To contact the author, go to:
Email: contactrmcknight@gmail.com
Instagram: sister.rumika

Kingdom Promise
Publishing
WHERE PURPOSE MEETS ...

DEDICATIONS

God has been and will always be the lamp of my life! I thank Him daily for giving me the Grace to live.

To my childhood friend Leona Bullard. You did not know those five little words you spoke to me in Summer 2016, "I Just Don't Get It!" help put this book in perspective for me, you, and others who would read it. I pray that after reading this, you "Get It" now! Love you bunches!

NOTE FROM THE AUTHOR

I do not expect this book to be the answer to all of your questions, but within this series lies a great deal of revelation, birth out of my journey and transition to a growing oneness with Christ. I tried my best to break the information down the best I could so you may gain understanding and stay connected to Christ. I do not expect you to read this section in a matter of days or weeks. My prayer and hope are that as you read through what is imparted, you will take frequent pauses and apply them to your life. Please do not just read through. Take your time, gain an understanding, and apply them. Nothing in your life will really change until you invest in the change that you want to become.

Soul Salvation

I JUST DON'T GET IT?

RUMIKA MCKNIGHT

TABLE OF CONTENTS

FOREWORD

How exactly can one live the Christian life? How do you break free from old habits? Where do you go for strength in the heat of the battle? These are very real everyday questions that Believers have and seek answers to as they walk through this Christian journey.

In the book, "I just don't get it" speaker, poet, and author Rumika E. Mcknight take you through her journey as she shares her testimony of God's mighty hand, love and dealings in her life. As she creatively takes you from chapter to chapter you can feel her heart, the passion that she has for the presence of God, as well as her desire for His people to be closer to Him in Spirit and in the truth of His Word. This read not only reveals the story of one who has been redeemed and washed in the blood of the Lamb but also provides each reader with nuggets of wisdom and tools necessary to live a strong and successful Christian life.

I have had the privilege and honor of knowing the author for over 30 years. I have seen her go through several stages of her process in God from attending youth group services with her all the way until now as she hosts women's events and oversees campaigns and projects. I have known her to be a loving, strong and loyal woman of God. We are friends, we are sisters, and we are family.

So, as you read this book, know that you are reading an authentic story of the love and power of God and how He changes lives. He did it for the author, He did for me and He is certainly able to do it for you.

Sherice Lanae Morris
Author and Christian Music Recording Artist

INTRODUCTION

I befriended a young lady in college. She was a Buddhist. To some our relationship seemed awkward. Once we were asked, "Do you know she's a Christian?" "Do you know she's a Buddhist?" The mere fact that we sat on a bench together having a conversation was incomprehensible in the mind of the young lady that asked. Now I will admit that I did speak to my Buddhist Friend about Jesus from time to time, and answered a few questions here and there, but I was not prepared to hear her tell me a few years later over a Facebook chat that she had given her life to the Lord and was faithfully attending a local church.

We lost touch.

One day while riding with a girlfriend of mine, I ran into my "Buddhist" friend in front of a local restaurant. I was excited to see her, and eager to hear how her walk with Christ was going. You can imagine my expression when she told me she'd stop attending the local church. She even went as far to say, "I'm not practicing Christianity no more, I've returned to Buddhism. It was too much." My heart fell to my stomach and I was at a loss for words. I had known the fights and obstacles she faced once she accepted Christ, but at that moment all I could say was,

"The attacks were real huh?"

"Yes!" she replied.

"That's how you know this is the real deal!" I said.

She understood.

What is Spiritual Warfare, and why is it so important for us as Christ Followers to understand it? The Apostle Paul sheds some light on the topic in the book of *2 Corinthians 10:3-5*

2

"For though we live in this world, we do not wage war as the world does. The weapons we [Christ Followers] fight with are not weapons of the world [physical things]. On the contrary, they have divine power to demolish strongholds. We demolish arguments and every pretension that sets itself up against the knowledge of God, and we take captive every thought to make it obedient to Christ." N.I.V

At that moment, what I said was probably not the most encouraging thing to say, but it was the truth. In order to understand this scripture, you must acknowledge that there is a spiritual realm in which we do not see, but yet it exists; and as Christ Followers we have authority in this realm through Christ Jesus.

Matthew 18:18 is evidence of this, Christ says,

"I tell you the truth, whatever you bind on earth will be bound in heaven, and whatever you loose on earth will be loosed in heaven." *(N.I.V.)*

What does Matthew 18:18 have to do with this situation and how does it relate to Spiritual Warfare? Christ was not speaking in a literal or physical sense of binding [tying down] and loosing [setting free], but He was speaking in a spiritual sense in a manner of prayer. Christ is saying, before anything takes place in the earthly (physical) realm it must first happen spiritually, and once it happens spiritually then it will be manifested physically. For example, you have an idea. Just because you have that idea doesn't mean that it is accessible to everyone else. It has to go through the proper channels of development, production, and manifestation, in order for others to utilize or fully understand its function. Once you have produced this idea then you will be able to reap the fruits of your labor.

In the Book of John Chapter 15, we know that Jesus is the vine, and we are the branches that produce fruit. The fruit that we produce is both spiritual and carnal. Galatians 5 gives us the Fruit of the Spirit. As long as we are connected to Jesus we are to grow in Love, Joy, Peace, Patience, Kindness, Goodness, Faithfulness, Gentleness, and Self- Control. Since we are carnal beings, and God is a god of balance, He wants us to prosper in every area of our life as well. As Believers, Christ Followers, Christians, in order to continuously produce these fruits which enables to grow in our spiritual [Christ maturity], we must stay connected and go through the proper channel, which is Jesus by way of the Holy Spirit.

Just like your idea, you will always face obstacles and people that will fight against you, deter, distract, or discourage you, so is it in the spiritual realm as it pertains to your fruit, and much more, your salvation. Spiritual Warfare is everything and so is everyone that arises against the knowledge and Word of God and tries to tear down, kill, steal, and or try to destroy your fruit, salvation.

From the days of John the Baptist until now, the kingdom of heaven has been subjected to violence, and violent people have been raiding it.

Matthew 11:12 N.I.V.

The thief comes only to steal and kill and destroy; I have come that they may have life and have it to the full.

John 10:10 N.I.V.

Let me tell you a story…

IT'S ME

It was early Spring of 2013, I was venturing on a seven day fast to seek God for wisdom in certain areas pertaining to my life. I was at, what felt like a dead end in my life; things just weren't working out right for me. I was in a relationship with my high school sweetheart, Ian, and our relationship was deteriorating by the day. We were arguing all the time because I was unhappy with myself and the lifestyle we were choosing to live. We were disagreeing about everything. Although I loved him deeply, he brought so much pain to my heart. At times, I remember the nights I spent crying myself to sleep and crying out to God to take the pain away from me. Despite our history, I prayed and asked God to change him or reveal to me if he was the one for me.

In May of the previous year, I graduated with my Associates in Arts Degree from a local community college. Around this time, I was finishing my last course in college, and preparing myself for the next step in my education, which was applying to nursing school. This turned me into a nerve wrecking mess. I was fearful. Although I did very well in my courses, I somehow felt not good enough and unsure of myself. Others believed in me more than I believed in myself. I put a lot of pressure on myself, stressing myself throughout the whole process.

During this time, I was also raising my two beautiful daughters, and helping Ian to raise his son. My eldest had just turned nine, my youngest was about to turn four, and his son had just turned three. I always knew that I was a good mother to the kids, but I wanted to be a great mom. I felt in my heart that there was more that I could offer them besides a home, necessities, and a mediocre love. At that moment I was thinking about their future a lot, not what they would become or accomplish, but who they would be spiritually. I knew how important a relationship with Christ is. I experienced a lot of challenges and setbacks in life and in my faith because I did not have a sound understanding of who Christ and God really were. I did not want my children to grow up with this same uncertainty. I prayed and asked God to help me to get myself together, so I could be the wholly (physically, emotionally, spiritually) mother for them.

I accepted Christ Jesus as my Lord and Savior at the age of seven. I was the typical child growing up in a first-generation Christian home. My mom was a Christian, although her parents were not. She gave her heart to Christ when she was fifteen years old but did not start living the lifestyle until she was in her mid-thirties, so there were a lot of things she herself did not understand. I can remember from an early age we were always in church, Sundays, Wednesdays, and if there was a revival, we were there every day as well.

I thought, asking Jesus to come into my heart was the gist of salvation and didn't require anything more besides following the Ten Commandments. I was brought up under a fire and brimstone theology. Everything, every choice, every action, every word, either led to heaven or hell. My mother's household was strict. I was not allowed to do anything. Christianity was so rigid and boring, and for that reason I resented it, because there was no enjoyment in my life. As I got older, I faltered and strayed away from my religion. I would back slide then reconcile, backslide then reconcile again.

At this period in my life, Spring of 2013, I was living out my faith in a relationship with God through Christ Jesus. I loved the Lord with all my heart. I had rededicated my life in June of 2011 and was baptized in July of 2012. Understanding now what I was not taught then, my salvation was the beginning of a relationship with God and not a onetime event. In understanding this, I was growing spiritually with God. He began using me in certain areas of my life to be a vessel through which He drew me and others to Him.

While I was in junior college, He placed it on my heart to start a Christian Bible club on my campus. We called it T.H.U.M.B (Together in Harmony Uniting Many Believers). We started off small then grew to a little community of ten to fifteen students who would meet weekly on campus. We worshiped, studied scripture, prayed for one another, and fellowshipped together. We even hosted clothes and food drives, in which the goods went to local charities or to an overseas country. God no doubt was showing us favor and love, as well as working in and through me.

However, after all that subsided and during this period of my life, after I was done with school, after the relationship I wanted so bad was now in pieces, I felt alone and lost. I had become complacent in my faith. My days had become a routine of waking up, sending the girls to school, and jumping back in bed, I was depressed. Growing tired of the everyday norm I wanted a change. My spirit felt empty, I knew something was missing — I was desperate to hear from Abba, my Heavenly Father, so I started my journey of fasting.

Throughout the fast I brought before the Lord my aching heart from a broken relationship. I also was seeking wisdom in which nursing program I should apply to, or if I should be going into nursing at all. Lastly, I fasted because I wanted to become a better mother, a better Christ Follower, and a better version of me.

Section One:
My Side of the Story

Well, we all know the saying, "There are three sides to a story. "Your side, their side, and the truth!"

Well, here's my side of the story. I started my fast on a Monday. I did a fraction of what is known as the Daniel Fast. I ate fruits, vegetables, and drank plenty of water and some fruit juice. That morning I got right into it. I sent the girls off to school, went back to my bedroom, popped a Donnie McClurkin CD in my DVD player, and knelt down in front of the television. I allowed the music to minister to me as I meditated. I kept two tracks on repeat, *Only You Are Holy* and *Agnus Dei*. After a few minutes, I let my request be made known to the Lord. I cried, and I wept. I apologized to God for the lifestyle I was living and vowed to Him that I would change. I prayed that He would give me the strength and desire to want to change. I poured out my heart before Him. All the hurt and pain that I was feeling from a broken heart and all the hurt I had caused Him. I can remember specifically asking Him to show me if this guy was the one for me.

After this, I prayed for direction in my life, my family, friends, and my children. Spending little less than two hours in His presence, when I got off my knees, I picked up my Bible, and read a few scriptures. After which, I started my day.

For the period I fasted, the routine practices of jumping back into the bed ceased; instead, I kept myself busy. When I was not praying, or reading my Bible, I would clean my house, organize anything, or run errands. With strong determination and focus I needed to stay busy and be strengthened in the Lord. Each time I entered fasting I always remembered this scripture,

Moreover, when ye fast, be not, as the hypocrites, of a sad countenance: for they disfigure their faces, that they may appear unto men to fast. Verily I say unto you, they have their reward. But thou, when thou fastest, anoint thine head, and wash thy face; That thou appear not unto men to fast, but unto thy

Father which is in secret: and thy Father, which seeth in secret, shall reward thee openly.

Matthew 6:16-18 K.J.V

This went on for the next several days. I would get up, send the girls off to school and then go before the Lord to start my day.

I am able to tell this story because THIS IS MY TESTIMONY on what God did in my life, and how He delivered me!!

I am an overcomer by the Blood of the Lamb, and the words of [MY TESTIMONY.]

Revelation 12:11

FRIDAY

Staying up to read the Word and meditate on the Lord resulted in me retiring to bed extremely late the previous night. As a matter of fact, this could have been gone on for several nights. I was definitely not getting enough sleep. I felt an alertness in my spirit, so I kept myself awake, praying, writing psalms, and writing songs. I'd also been writing ideas that came to me concerning business ventures that would not only support me and my family financially, but also ways that I could serve God in my community and city, while spreading the Gospel.

Today was different for me though, I sensed it. Although I was operating on little sleep, I somehow felt energized and on the go. Ian was over, and I was discussing with him my fast during the week. Today I was telling him how I was rededicating my life back to Christ, and how God had been working in me, giving me the heart to change. We had also been discussing our relationship. I wanted us to consecrate ourselves and our relationship before the Lord since we had honestly been discussing marriage. We were never able to see eye to eye about consecration. I felt that it was a necessity for all believers to do, and over the past couple years had come to accept that once I gave my life to Christ, I would have to give up my secular lifestyle. Him, being a newly confessed Christian, this was hard for him to accept and do. I showed him 1 Corinthians 6:18-19, which talks about sexual immorality, and how it displeases God. I wanted us to become abstinent together. I thought if we took this journey together, it would somehow draw us closer together and closer to God. He did not agree with me. He loathed the idea. He reacted like I told him I was going to chop off his arms and a leg. He told me God only wanted me to be abstinent because I was previously married, but never formally divorced; and

11

being abstinent did not apply to him. Even if I was to become abstinent, he would respect that, but he would still go about having intercourse, just not with me. I felt pressured.

We went back and forth for an hour discussing the Word of God and bickering about who it applied to. I tried to tell him that this applies to all believers, but for some strange reason I did not understand, he felt that it did not apply to him. He was like many Christians, and me, who picked and chose what part of the Bible we should obey. Nevertheless, we could not come to a common ground about consecrating our relationship, so we ended the debate.

As I thought to myself, I was disappointed, hurt, betrayed, and even more upset. I was left to decide if I had enough courage to do this journey on my own, and I feared losing him. I was wavering between two choices, would I give in to his belief even though I knew it was wrong, and continue to have sex with him going against the will and Word of God and God Himself, or should I do what I know is right, what God has commanded me to do.

I cannot remember the exact time frame, it could have been minutes, maybe an hour, but we were now in my bedroom by now. I was still angry with him. I could not understand why he didn't understand what the Bible said about living in fornication. Still upset that he would not make that sacrifice with me and live-in consecration before God.

There was a wooden table in my bedroom. His brother had made it in woodshop many years prior. I fell in love with this table the first time I saw it. It was simple, but unique. It reminded me of picnic tables at the park. It stood about a foot and a half off the ground. It was unpainted when I first saw it, so I went to Walmart and bought some tan spray paint and painted it. In the front, there is a board that went horizontal connecting the legs. I decorated it with a collage of smooth stones and vase gems. I did the same with the backboard as well, except I put our initials on it. It was beautiful!

Okay, back to the story. On this table I had many of my belongings on it, it was ridiculous. I would walk in my bedroom and whatever was in my hand got thrown on this table. Well, Ian had acquired quite a few of his belongings on this table as well, and around my bedroom. In a split second, something came over me, and I began to take everything off the table and erratically began throwing them onto my bed. I then looked around my bedroom for the rest of his belongings and threw them on the bed too. As I'm doing this, we hear an ice cream truck passing by, and he gets up to go buy the kids ice cream from the truck. He returned a few minutes later to a heap of what looked like a mess piled on the bed. He was shocked, and I was a mad woman. Then I asked him to help me to separate the pile into two smaller piles. Mine and his. We began, and after several minutes had passed, he turned, looked at me, and asked,

"Are you ok?" I replied,

"Yes, and that we just needed to finish this". I continued separating the pile, speaking after I lifted one item after another.

"Not mine. Not mine. Mine. Mine. Not mine.".

Throwing the items in their designated piles. When we were done, I told him to look at the two piles. I said something along the lines of,

"You don't want to do this together then we must separate, here's your stuff and here is mine."

As I was saying this to him, I was visualizing a separation. Not a physical separation, but a spiritual separation, the breaking of a

13

soul tie. I did not express this to him. At the time, I did not know or understand what I saw.

I gave him a black garbage bag to put all his belongings in. When he had done that, I had somehow convinced him to lie down on the floor. I began praying over him, anointing him with oil, and moving my hands up and down his body. As I was doing this, I told him that God wants to purify him and cleanse him. There was an iron nearby, I grabbed it. I hovered it up and down over his body, telling him that God wants to straighten him out. He laid there for a while and a few minutes later he became freaked out! So, he got up.

"Are you okay?" He asked.

"This is beginning to get weird and it's overwhelming me. You're piling things on the bed, praying, and all the things you keep saying. I'm not gonna lie, you're scaring me!"

He grabbed his keys and headed for the door. I was right behind him, begging him not to leave, telling him that we should stick together, but he insisted on leaving. He kissed my forehead, told me he loved me and that he would return, then he left.

His sister was in town visiting for the weekend. She had heard our debate earlier but did not see what happened behind the closed door of my bedroom. I went to her for comfort and asked her for her opinion on our situation. She is a subtle girl, but very direct when it comes to speaking her mind. She expressed to me that her brother had always been stubborn. She told me that she understood how much I loved him; we had known each other for fourteen years.

"No matter how much you love a person, you will never be able to change them. In the end, you will just end up hurting yourself." she said to me.

By this time, it was late. The sun had gone down, and the kids had taken their nightly baths. I was in an emotional turmoil and could not think straight. My thoughts were racing a thousand miles per minute, and I could not get a hold of myself. I was pacing back and forward in my bedroom. I would walk in one direction and think, it's over between me and him. What am I going to do, gripping my chest? I would walk in the other direction, thinking to myself, not this time, I cannot do this to God again. I kept thinking about my relationship, and how it was basically over. My thoughts shifted back to God, and the reason why I was doing this fast, committing myself back to Him. It would require me to let this guy go. Spiritually, we were not equal.

Be ye not unequally yoked together with unbelievers [Those that do not agree with the Word of God]: for what fellowship hath righteousness with unrighteousness? and what communion hath light with darkness?

2 Corinthians 6:14 N.I.V.

Oh Lord! I literally began to lose it. After about forty-five minutes, I thought to myself, I need to calm down. My mind was shifting back and forth between loving God enough to obey him or holding onto something I had cherished and made an idol. I was in disarray. I needed to smoke. Two weeks prior to this fast I had not smoked one joint; I had my heart set on quitting. I was about to break that streak. I did not have any cash on me and did not feel like driving to the ATM for money, so I asked my sister- in- law for six dollars. Five dollars to buy me a sack and a dollar to buy me a blunt. She gave it to me, and I texted my weed man and he brought me a sack, then I headed to the store to buy me a Chocolate Dutch. When I got back, I went to my room and rolled my joint.

I just Don't Get it?

It was a little before eleven o'clock; I sat on my bed, next to that pile, and smoked. I thought to myself, this would calm me down, allow me to get my thoughts in order or maybe even sleep.

I barely smoked half of the joint. I was hoping it would help me cope better with the situation. I did calm down; well, my emotions did. My erratic behavior however did not stop. I paced around my townhouse for I don't know how long. Then when I wanted to lie down, I could not. My pile of belongings was still on my bed. Instead, I went downstairs to grab me something to eat. I was starting to get the munchies. The marijuana was kicking in my system and I was beginning to get an appetite.

It was now nearing sunrise, and Ian had not returned. I'd been texting and calling him. I kept getting his voicemail and he was not responding to my text messages. I left him numerous voice messages. I began pacing the house again, going from room to room. I went to the room where his sister was sleeping and told her that I was going to look for him. She insisted on me not going. She told me that she was worried about me. She said I was not behaving like myself, and I should lie down and get some sleep. I insisted on going out. I told her what to feed the kids for breakfast, told her I loved her, then I left.

SATURDAY

When I left the house, inwardly I was a mess, in so much turmoil emotionally and spiritually. Outwardly I was the complete opposite. I felt like my poise was calm as I casually and slowly walked to my car when I felt like running. I was wearing a yellow tube top, a pair of gray slacks, and loafers. It was cold out, so I grabbed my leather high school jacket, and a small cotton blanket that I draped over my head.

In one hand, I had a mini pink steam trunk that Ian had bought me as a gift. In the steam trunk, I placed all the jewelry and little trinkets that he had bought me over the course of two years. In my other hand, I had my Coach bag, which he also bought me as a gift for having a good semester in school, and in it was my Bible and a bottle of olive oil. I threw the steam trunk in the back of my Volvo station wagon and got behind the wheel. Lord lead me to him, I prayed.

I remembered that a friend of mine, let's call her Stacy, mentioned to me that she saw him on a certain side of town at another girl's house. She would not tell me where, but she gave me a street name. As I drove to the area, I was praying. I felt God was leading me there, so I began to follow the directions in my head. I was led to an apartment complex. Then to the rear of the complex, which was literally a DEAD END. Seriously, it had the metal barricades with the yellow reflective diamond shaped signs in all. That should have been a sign to me, but I ignored it and pressed on. I got out of the car, threw my cell phone and keys in the back inside the steam trunk with the rest of my things, and carried my purse.

I began to walk. I first went down this dirt path that was adjacent to a canal on the outskirts of the complex. As I was walking, the sun was rising, and I felt at peace. I forgot all about trying to find Ian. I felt like I was walking in the presence of the Lord. I was completely oblivious to everything that was going on around me. I began to sing. The first song I sang was, Now Behold the Lamb by Kirk Franklin. I sang the chorus but could only remember one particular part of the song,

"When I always didn't do right. I went left, and you told me to go right. Now I'm standing right here in the midst of my tears, I claim you to be the Lamb of

God."

This song was in my spirit, so I sang it repeatedly. Again, if I had been coherent, I would have paid attention to the lyrics of this song and took it as a sign to me, but as I was incoherent, completely oblivious to everything including myself.

I'm off the path now, and it led me to a sidewalk that ran parallel on the back side of the apartment complex. As I am walking, I hear another song in my spirit. It was so melodic; I've never heard anything like it before. I began to sing it,

You are my Rock, my King

You are my Rock, my King You are, You are

I'll give You everything Your praises I will sing You are, You are.

God had not blessed me with a singing voice, but the words flowed from my belly as I belted them out. I was surprised that my voice could sound so sweet. I'm walking and I'm singing.

It's early morning and there was hardly anyone outside. I was led into the apartment complex through a side entrance. As I'm walking the complex, I could remember scanning to see if I spotted

18

Ian's car. While I was scanning, something came over me, and I felt led to begin to knock on doors, and minister to the inhabitants of the apartment. The first door, no one answered. I knocked on the next one.

I heard the locks, and then the door opened. Lo and behold, it was my weed man! I was thrown aback. He was the last person that I expected to see that morning.

When I got past my shock, I greeted him Good Morning, and asked if I may step in. The house was dimly lit from the sun as I entered, and he ushered me to a couch. He told me that this was his sister's house, he had come here the night before to visit her. She was still in the back room sleeping. I began to speak to him. A part of me wanted to ask him, if he knew where Ian was, but the spirit led me to tell him about my marijuana habit, and how I had been trying to quit, although I just bought a bag from him last night. That must've been a shocker for him. Here I am one of his regular customers, telling him that I need to stop purchasing his product, but he was very understanding.

Next, I began to share my faith with him. I expressed to him how I firmly believe in Christ Jesus, and what salvation in Christ meant to me. I expressed to him how important it was to have a relationship with God, and how to strengthen that relationship by reading the Bible, which is God's Word. He informed me that he did read the Bible from time to time. He grew up in the church, so he understood everything spoken. I asked him if he had a Bible handy. He got up and went to the back room, he returned with one, and I asked him to turn to *1 Corinthians 6:9-10* as I pulled out my Bible, and we read it together.

Do you not know that the unrighteous will not inherit the Kingdom of God? Do not be deceived: neither the sexually immoral, idolaters, nor adulterers, nor men who practice homosexuality, nor thieves, nor the greedy, nor drunkards, nor revilers, nor the swindlers, will inherit the Kingdom of God. N.I.V

I explained to him that our relationship with God is very important. These verses imply to us that not everyone will make it to heaven, but we have the choice to turn away from our sin and rely on God to do the work in us. I gave him comfort and told him that I was not judging him, because I would have to judge myself and neither of us was perfect. Then I asked him if he'd allow me to pray for him. He obliged, so I took his hand, and prayed for him and myself. When I was done, he thanked me then I left.

I did not feel the need to continue going from door to door, I cannot recall if I had been discouraged or if I was satisfied, having been able to pray with my weed man. I walked and walked. By this time, I was exhausted and barefooted because I abandoned my shoes at a different apartment complex I walked through. My car was literally two blocks away, but it never crossed my mind to go back to my car and head home. I was out doing the "Lord's work", this was more important.

MR. AND MRS. DALE

I'd just met Mr. and Mrs. Dale, owners of a local barber shop and beauty salon, a few weeks earlier, when I took Ian's son to get a haircut. I said to myself, "Well, I can go there." I headed to their shop which was at least forty minutes away in walking distance. They were a young couple, and the shop was their business. We hit it off quite nicely the first time I visited the shop, and I had dropped in from time to time just to say hello.

When I finally got there, I was greeted by their perplexed faces. They were probably thrown off by the way I was dressed, or maybe my thin body. I lost a substantial amount of weight. I immediately expressed my need to lie down in the back room they use to keep their kids entertained. Mrs. Dale walked me to the back room and continued asking me if I was okay. I simply told her that I was tired and needed to rest.

I laid down and put the sheet I draped over me earlier that morning, over my head to block out the light. I do not know how long I was there, trying to sleep before I got up to use the bathroom, and went back to lie down.

After about a half an hour, Mrs. Dale returned to check up on me and asked me if I was up to braiding a client's hair. Since I could not sleep, I told her that I didn't mind doing it. The client was Terry. I had met Terry before, when she visited Mrs. Dale for a consultation. When she arrived, I began braiding her hair while all three of us indulged in girl chat. I felt well, but a little distracted as I tried a new braiding style on her hair. A couple of hours could have passed, and it was the Dale's closing time. Terry and I decided that we would go to her house and finish with her hair.

TERRY

As we were driving to her house, she too asked me how I was feeling. She expressed to me that I didn't look well and that I had lost a lot of weight. She asked me when was the last time that I ate. I told her I had been fasting. "How long have you been fasting?"

"Since March 4th".

"Do you know today's date?" she exclaimed. I told her I did not, and she then told me it was the 23rd. "You have not eaten in nineteen days!" she remarked, and I counted the days on my fingers.

I sat there, in the passenger seat, trying to understand her shock. Then it hit me, I started out on a seven day fast, and here I am three weeks later still fasting, and I did not even know it! I thought to myself, God must have really gotten a hold of me.

Somewhere in me, I kind of felt pride in that, I was almost at a benchmark of twenty-one days, and it seemed like a piece of cake to me. On the other hand, I tried to figure out when I lost track of time. How could that amount of time pass and I had no consciousness of it. She took me to Subway to buy me lunch, insisting I eat something. When we got there, I went inside while she stayed in the car.

When I returned with the food, I felt spiritually elevated. There was a clarity, a pureness that I was experiencing, but I could not explain. The best description I can give is that everything I saw, I experienced it through the eyes of someone or something else.

We had reached her place. As I sat down at her dining room table, I drank some of the soup that she purchased from Subway for me. I tried to eat the sandwich, but I couldn't, my body rejected it. After I'd drank the soup, I told her I was ready to finish her hair. I got a couple of braids in, and suddenly had the urge to go to the restroom. I told Terry, and for some reason, I cannot remember, she escorted me to the bathroom then waited outside the door. I went to the bathroom, sat on the toilet, and relieved myself. With my pants on.

I must've been in there for some time. Terry knocked on the door and asked me if I was doing okay. I told her I had an accident, and she entered the bathroom, with me standing there bare bottomed. She was so patient and sincere, as she brought me a towel, and a change of clothes, including a pair of new underwear she had. As I washed up and changed, she began to clean the floor. At a time when I should have felt shame and embarrassment, I was not embarrassed at all. I was calm and felt at ease as she catered to me and helped me to get cleaned up.

We went back into the dining area, where I was doing her hair. Her husband brought me a Bible and he gave me a note with a list of Psalms on it, and it said, "Pray for seven days." Then he went away. I'm not sure where she went, but I began to feel uneasy and very paranoid, and thought to myself, this is the time I can "escape". While they weren't paying attention, I grabbed my purse, exited out the front door, and began to run as fast as I could.

I sprinted around the corner and halfway down the next block, behind their home. I stopped when I noticed a father and son outside doing some yard work. I approached them and asked if they had a cell phone, I could use to make a phone call. I called Ian. I gave him my location and asked him to pick me up. He reassured me he was on his way. I thanked the father and son duo for their generosity, and continued down their street towards the main road, where I told Ian to pick me up. When I got to the main road, I waited. I noticed a short stone wall, I sat on it. I was there for about thirty minutes before I spotted Terry, driving by, no doubt looking for me. "What happened?" she asked. "I had to get out of there." I replied.

"Did I do something wrong?"

"No, I just had to leave."

She pleaded with me to get inside the car, so she could take me home. I felt very unbalanced around her. Something in me was skeptical about trusting her. Whatever was going on inside me was beginning to manifest, as my demeanor and behavior began to change. I started crying and yelling at her. Yet she was so patient with me. The gentleness in her voice and the calmness of her spirit allowed me to return to tranquility. I cannot remember our dialog, but suddenly I was kneeling before her and begging her to bless me, placing her hand on my head. She kept speaking reassuring words towards me, as she helped me up off the ground and into her vehicle. Just as I got up, we saw Ian speed by.

"Ian!"

I yelled and jumped into her vehicle. I was jumping up and down in my seat, like a child getting ready to go to the candy store, yelling at her to follow him. For some reason, I kept telling her he was going to the church, and we were going to get married.

"It's okay baby, it's okay, I'm going to take you home." Terry said as we made a U-turn and headed to my apartment.

KAMILAH

I cannot remember most of the drive back to my apartment. I do remember talking to Terry about my friend Kamilah. As it turned out they both attended the same church, but never met one another. I asked her to take me to Kamilah's house, so I could speak with her and she said no.

Since Kamilah and I lived in the same apartment complex, I would dupe her into taking me there anyway. We pulled into my apartment complex, and I led her to Kamilah's apartment instead of mine. When we parked, I told her I would be right back. I somehow had pulled myself together, and I was not as agitated as I was fifteen minutes' prior, however I still did not feel like myself. It was like I was outside my body, watching myself act. She suddenly figured out that I had lied to her, and she got out of the car and followed me up the stairs trying to persuade me to not speak with her.

When Kamilah opened the door, I waltzed in-side of her apartment, as if I were a detective from one of them CSI shows. I somehow felt that she was hiding something from me. Whatever it was, I was going to find out. I went straight to her bathroom without even asking her permission. As I was washing my hands, I can remember looking into her bathroom mirror and laughing wickedly.

I came out of the bathroom, walked over to her dining room table, and stood there. I asked her how she was doing, and then we had a short conversation about keeping in touch with some of the members from T.H.U.M.B. When the small talk was done, I looked her in her eyes, and asked her if there was something that she had to tell me. She looked puzzled as she responded,

"Like what?"

"Is there something you have to tell me?" I retorted. And she replied,

"No!" I asked her one last time, then she fell to her knees with her hands in the air and yelled,

"Jesus!"

When she yelled Jesus, I felt a shift within me; it was like I was someone else. She cupped her stomach and wept, kneeling on the floor. When I looked back at her I saw her in a vision. There was fire all around her, she was reaching out to me, begging me, saying, "Sorry, Sorry, don't leave me!"

At that moment, I felt like we were partaking in the rapture, and Kamilah was getting left behind. Then there was another shift. I looked at Kamilah and told her it was okay. I forgave her. Then she stood up, I saw her, envisioned in white, pure, she shone. I began to laugh; it felt like we had just defeated Satan. I looked at them both, and said, (Excuse the language please.) "We three bad **expletive**!"

As I stood there, I heard Terry say to Kamilah,

"Is she ever like this?"

"No, No." she cried out.

I paid them no mind as I grabbed my purse and headed out of Kamilah's apartment.

FINALLY, HOME

The sun was beginning to set as I finally allowed Terry to take me home. We got in the car, and she reversed. My house was less than a minute away. A deep fear began to come over me as I begged her not to leave me. She said to me, "God will never leave you or forsake you."

I begged her to promise me that SHE would never leave me repeatedly. She finally gave in and made me that promise. We pulled up to my door, but she did not park. I looked at her with sorrowful eyes and asked her, why she had not parked. She told me that she was coming back to park and got out to walk me to the door. I cannot recall how we got on the subject, but we were talking about cleaning my house. We went inside, and she told me to stay in the house.

"Clean your house and take care of your babies." She said.

She turned around to leave, and I ran after her, again begging her to stay. She turned around and asked me to bring her something from inside my house (I don't remember what it was.), so I ran upstairs to grab it for her. When I returned with the things, she was gone. I can remember being hurt, calling her crying; telling her she broke her promise to me, never to leave me or forsake me.

I was back to pacing once again, this time I was trembling horribly. I felt so afraid, and very, very paranoid. I somehow managed to get the kids fed, and in bed. I commenced cleaning my house. I washed the dishes, cleaned the kitchen, swept, and mopped the living room, and then headed upstairs. I cleaned the kid's bathroom then moved to my bedroom and bathroom. As I was cleaning my bathroom, I kept hearing clean and unclean, so I grabbed the bleach and bleached everything down. When I was done, I still heard unclean, so I emptied the garbage, swept, and mopped the floor, and cleaned the mirrors. I still heard unclean. By this time, I am frustrated and confused. The bleach was burning my nostrils, and I had cleaned everything possible that could be cleaned.

"Unclean, unclean, unclean!"

I kept hearing it, until I ripped down the shower curtain, took everything off the countertops, took the garbage out, and put out a fresh roll of toilet paper, then shut the bathroom door. I stood in front of the bathroom door looking at my room, which was a mess. The pile of mess was still on the bed, papers and notebooks were all over the floor, along with clothes and shoes. I was overwhelmed by the uncleanliness and chaos that was now in my bedroom. I went back downstairs and began pacing again.

THE BURNS

It was about ten o'clock Saturday night by this time. I was at the door to one of my neighbor's house; we will call them the Burns. With my children by my side. I left Ian's sister and his son at my apartment. I'm not sure if she even knew that I had left with the kids. My gosh I was so paranoid, I cannot remember what I told them, but Mr. Burns let us into their apartment. I was high strung and stammering and acting very panicky. I told them that I needed to make a phone call. He handed me their cordless phone, seconds later I was calling the police.

When I dialed 911, the operator answered, and I became filled with an intense amount of fear and paranoia. I kept looking over my shoulder as I cradled the phone in my hand. I began to beg the operator to dispatch officers to my location because I was in fear for my life. I told her that my boyfriend threatened to kill me because I found out he was cheating on me, and I threatened to leave him. I knew that was not true, and honestly the lie just rolled off my tongue. I couldn't believe I said it, but once it was said, I held it as the truth.

The operator stayed on the phone with me, and the officers were there in less than ten minutes. When the officers knocked on the door, I went outside to speak with them. I cannot remember much about the conversation, but I convinced them to take me to my church. I told them someone there was expecting me, which wasn't true, but I needed to tell them something of that nature to persuade them to take me there. It was cold outside that night, and Mr. Burns lent me a white sweat jacket. I trusted him and his family, so I left my children with them, while the officers took me to the church.

HELP!

When they dropped me to the church, the workers were there cleaning up after a Saturday night's service and all the doors were locked. I stood by the church door peering inside trying to get someone's attention, but no one walked by. My intention was to speak to someone about what was going on with me, and to get prayer. By this time, I knew that something was going on with me. The voices I was hearing, the things I was doing; I was confused, afraid, and paranoid; but I was fighting. I didn't understand how serious it was, but I needed the church to pray over me.

There was a woman and a young lady outside in a car, waiting for a relative to get off. I approached them and told them why I was at the church. I also told them I attended the church regularly. I asked them if they would get in contact with their relative on the inside and find out if he can get an administrator from the church to come outside to talk and pray with me. They made the phone call, but when the gentleman came outside, he gave me the cold shoulder and treated me as if I had leprosy. I tried to explain to him, I needed prayer. When he resisted getting me the help, I asked him and his family to pray with me. Over and over, I pleaded with them. He gave me a look of disgust, cradled his family, directed them into the church, and locked the doors.

I cried. The church had now turned its back on me, in my darkest hour of need. This was my last hope, and now I didn't know what to do. Looking back to this moment, I believe this was the straw that broke the camel's back. I lost it. Now I was completely given over to my mind, and the dark spirit, which tormented me.

I was frantic, as I began to walk around the outside of the church. Paranoid, continually looking over my shoulders, as if I were being followed. I remembered a seven-eleven being further down the road, about twenty minutes walking distance. I set off, walking in that direction.

When I got there, I spoke with the attendant who allowed me to use the store's phone to contact Terry. I had her number written on a small piece of paper in my purse. I called her and asked her to come and pick me up. She questioned me on how I ended up on that side of town, and she would send someone to come and get me.

After about fifteen minutes of not seeing her, I called her back. She reassured me someone was coming to get me. I asked her to stay on the phone with me until they arrived. I was bugging out in fear and paranoia. I told her I had the urge to smoke and asked her if I may smoke marijuana. She told me no. I then asked her if I could smoke a cigarette, she said yes. I had never smoked a cigarette before this day and did not know where I was going to get one from.

I walked outside and sat on the ground leaning against the building. I was sitting there for a little while, alone, until a homeless man came and approached me and started speaking to me. He was drunk. I can remember smelling the stench of alcohol coming off him. He pulled out a cigarette and began to smoke. I asked him for a cigarette, and he gave me two. We sat there on the floor, backs against the wall having a conversation. He was ranting and raving about god knows what, and I was trying to talk to him about Christ.

We must have been there for twenty minutes talking, when three cop cars pulled up, the officers got out and approached us. They took the gentleman aside and began questioning him. They came to me, very sincere, and concerned. An officer approached me and asked me for my name, and then confirmed it with the dispatcher, whom he spoke with through the walkie on his shoulder. He then asked me a series of questions, kind of like the ones that nurses ask patients to test their coherence and alertness level. I can remember him asking me the date and year, which I answered to his satisfaction. He told me that Terry called them for me because she was worried about me. He then asked me who is Ian. I told him my fiancé. I don't remember the whole conversation between him and I, but in my mind, I was somewhere else.

I can remember thinking that they were there to take me back to the church to get married, and Ian had planned a big surprise wedding for me. I also can remember thinking that the rapture had happened that night, and I had gotten left behind, and it was my mission to preach the gospel. Like I mentioned my mind was all over the place. I must have expressed this to the officer because he began to ask me questions which led to evidence that the rapture had not taken place. He also told me he was a Christian, and so was the officer who stood next to him. He began to quote to me Biblical verses describing what the world would be like if the rapture had taken place, and asked me to look around, and look at the sky. He convinced me the rapture had not taken place, especially if they were still here. They were that confident in their faith. He then told me he was not taking me to the church to get married, because there was no one there. He was there to take me home. A few moments later after they sorted out the technicalities, I was in the back of the police cruiser on my way home.

SUNDAY: PHASE ONE

It was a little after midnight when the officers and I arrived at my home. They escorted me to the Burn's apartment to pick up my children, and then walked us home. I have a vague memory of what took place next. I did not go to sleep, and I can't remember how I spent the next several hours.

It was now about six in the morning, and I was up praying, specifically praying for my eldest daughter. She was born with Spina Bifida, and a congenital amputation that left her with one leg. I woke up all the children and Ian's sister and called them downstairs. I had them all sit in the center of my area rug in the living room. I remember being overzealous and very adamant. Talking about God, healing, and family. I grabbed my phone and I called Ian. He did not answer. I called him repeatedly, leaving him message after message. My messages remained unanswered.

SUNDAY: PHASE TWO

By this time, I felt completely out of myself, almost what I had experienced at Kamilah's house, but more intense. All control of my mind, my actions, my words, were not of my doing. I was experiencing and watching myself go through something I could not understand nor stop. I opened my front door and walked outside. I felt like I was experiencing heaven on earth. Everything felt different, clean, pure. I heard a voice say to me, "This is all yours, the earth is renewed, there is no more sin, no more death, no more sickness. Enjoy it, now you can relax."

I ran to the field behind my apartment building, my youngest daughter followed me, as I spun around in the field. I felt joy. I rolled around in the grass for a few minutes, then I laid there. There were children as well as my youngest daughter, playing at the nearby playground. The voice returned to me,

"These are your children, love all of them."

I started to run towards them to embrace them. My daughter ran up to me and gave me a hug. As I continued to make my way to the playground my demeanor changed, and I was frightened. I stopped in my tracks and started yelling obscenities at everyone in the area.

I ran back towards the direction of my apartment. When I got to the front of my apartment building, Mr. Burns was standing outside. When I saw him, it was not him I saw. I was looking at him, gut in my mind he had taken on the personification of God. He called me to him and looked at me with his deep gray eyes.

He spoke calming words to me, then I became quiet. He then told me he loved me, and he knew I had been hurt in my young life, and that I was hurting now. He mentioned to me he had a surprise for me, and it was behind one of the apartment doors he began to point to. He implied it was about my eldest daughter, and her being restored with two legs. He could heal her, but he needed me to stop holding onto something. At that moment, another one of neighbors walked up, Ms. Brittany, and joined the conversation. Mind you, when I had spoken to Mr. Burns and Ms. Brittany, their recollection of these events was totally different than mine. The story continues…

I was hesitant in talking around her; he reassured me it was alright for her to be there, and I could trust her. Standing there before them I felt like I was in the presence of holiness. When I looked at her again, I saw her differently, she looked divine. I cannot remember what she was wearing, but I saw her dressed in all white. We all began to discuss this surprise Mr. Burns, God, had for me, but for it to take place I had to let something go I was holding onto, or it would not work.

I began to think about what I would have to do; I was sure it had to do with me being able to trust him, God, fully. I began to question him, I asked him about Ian. He told me in my heart I knew the decision I had to make, and he would not influence me into making the decision. I debated with him then asked him to give me a few days to figure it out.

He said, "No!"

He became frustrated with me, and he and Ms. Brittany walked away towards her car. I hurried behind them, asking for a moment, a few hours to get myself ready for this. I explained to him letting Ian go was a very difficult thing for me to do. I was too attached to him, and I needed to prepare my heart for this. I did not have time, he told me, and it must be now. He told me I could not have both, Ian and whatever he had waiting for me behind the door. I had to choose, and in choosing I had to trust him. He stood looking at me, waiting for me to give him an answer. He became impatient, and they got in the car and began to reverse out the parking spot. He was done with me. I panicked. I began to yell and scream, "No, No. Don't leave me. I'll do it!"

They were driving away, when I jumped on the hood of the car, begging, and screaming for them not to leave me. Ms. Brittany stopped the car. I got off and they drove away. I stood there in the parking lot, pacing back and forth. I kept telling myself they will come back, and I can give him my final answer, but it did not feel that way. I felt a painful separation, like my covering, my protection, my security was gone. I felt like something terrible was about to happen to me, and I had no one and nothing to protect or defend me. I ran after him to show him that I was ready, I was willing to do what he wanted, and I would trust him. I cut across the playground to catch them before they exited the complex. I was too late. I had failed. I sat on the grass by the entrance, rocking, trying to contain myself, and contemplate my next move. My heart was palpitating heavily in my chest. I sat there screaming for them to come back. Screaming I would do anything, and I was ready now. I can remember taking off my shirt as a sign to him I had no shame, and I did not care about others opinion just His. I began to undress right then and there to get "God's" attention. I stopped when I went to take off my pants, put my shirt back on and ran back to my apartment.

SUNDAY: PHASE THREE

Of course, I was frantic when I entered the apartment, ranting and behaving erratically. I can remember Ian's sister telling me I was scaring the children, and they were all beginning to cry. I can remember walking hastily throughout the whole house, I was speaking about something, but I do not remember what I spoke of. I remember picking up the phone and calling my church. I wanted to speak with someone. I needed to speak with someone. When the secretary answered the phone, I was mumbling about speaking with the young adult's pastor. I believed I told her something was wrong with me, and I did not know what it was. When she told me he was not available, I demanded to speak with the head pastor. She tried calming me down while she asked me, what was the phone call about. I just kept telling her I needed to speak to him, and I didn't want to share any information with her, because my life depended on it, her life depended on it, his life depended on it. I believe she hung up on me.

I called back and reintroduced myself and told her I needed to speak with the pastor again. By this time, I think she realized I was not well, she tried to calm me down again. I hung up the phone, still pacing. I felt full of rage. I was going deeper into this trance. Everything began to happen in flashes. I walked outside and began screaming to the top of my lungs. Repent! Repent! God is coming, you all need to repent, or you are going to hell. I went back inside my house. I grabbed a broom and started beating on all my neighbor's doors and cars, screaming for them to come outside, and repent.

I remember seeing a crowd of children and a few adults standing in front of me. They looked as if they were laughing at me, as I was outside ranting and raving, creating a scene. I don't know how long that went on, but I remember police cars pulling up, and the officers jumping out of their cars screaming at me. I was furious and out of control as I cursed them and yelled obscenities at them. The next thing I knew I was in the back of the police car. Handcuffed. Naked.

I remember the officer going to his trunk, retrieving a pink cotton bathrobe, and throwing it over me to cover my body. When he got in the car, I was very apologetic to him. I was talking to him and asking him to please take me to the church. I needed to get to the church. He nodded his head at me and kept quiet. He paid me no attention. I asked him if he was a Christian, and he said yes. I told him I was a Christian as well. Then I told him to let the Spirit lead him, I was not going to tell him where to take me. I laid down in the back seat, and I fell asleep.

When I awoke, I was surrounded by three men in medical uniforms and the police officer. I was at a mental institute. I had a full-blown mental breakdown. I had lost my mind....

DEEP BREATH...

I know I need one, after recounting these events to shed light on this topic. I spent seventy-two hours in lock up as per protocol while they "nursed" me back to health. During this time, I was sent to a local hospital for a few hours to receive fluids and eat, I was very dehydrated and malnourished. They performed several drug tests on me through urine samples and kept a close eye on me. I was blessed with such a wonderful nurse who went over and beyond the call of duty. She spoke to me with understanding; she even gave me her testimony about her being in an analogous situation at one point in her life. When I was healthy enough, they shipped me back to the mental institute.

For the first thirty-six some odd hours, I still battled within myself. It wasn't until halfway through the second day I began to return somewhat back to normal.

The night before, I picked up the Gideon New Testament Bible which they had scattered throughout the whole building. It included the Book of Psalms, I read through it with intensity. My spirit had a hunger for the Word, and I read it throughout the day, or whenever we had "free time". Later that day I had a scheduled appointment with the facility's Nurse Practitioner discussing my release for the following day.

During the meeting, the Nurse Practitioner discussed with me the purpose of me being there, and the terms of my release. Upon me walking into her office, she commented on my demeanor, telling me I looked like a totally different person from the person who was brought in a couple of days prior. She asked me if I remembered speaking to her the first day, in which I replied, no. She recounted my first few hours there by telling me how out of it

I was, and they had to put me down with a shot of Demerol. I remember the shot; it took about four staff members to hold me down while a R.N. administered the shot in my bottom!

She then brought up my drug test and told me that it came back positive. I admitted to it and told her that I did smoke marijuana a couple of days prior. She knew that because she had my drug test results. She then asked me what other drugs I had been taking. I looked at her puzzled. Other drugs? I told her I never experimented with other drugs before, only marijuana. She told me, the reason she asked was because the type of behavior I displayed was from either another type of drug or a deeper-rooted issue. She had never seen anyone flip out to that extent on marijuana. She went through a list of drugs I could have taken, but would not show up on the drug test, and I replied no to them all. She then asked me about my mental history, and my family's mental history; having found nothing there, and seeing my improvement, she agreed to let me go home the next day under an outpatient psychiatric care.

For the next several months I tried to recover from what was now being called "my episode". The psychiatrist I was seeing put me on psychiatric medication; however, he could not diagnose me. One month he called it schizophrenia, the next month it was bipolar, and the next month it was manic depression. After six months, and no proper diagnosis, I made the decision to stop seeing him.

I relived my episode day after day for months. The more I tried to put it out of my mind, the more I thought about it. I prayed, and I cried out to God for months, day after day, asking Him what happened to me? Why did this happen to me? I fell into a deeper depression than I was before. Not only that, but my mind was in disarray. I lost friends and their respect, some of my family members stopped talking to me, and the medication that was supposed to be helping me made me feel worse and zombified me.

I searched for revelation with people I respected in ministry. I knew what I went through was deeper than drugs and a medical diagnosis. I shared my story with them, and none of them could explain to me or give me insight into what happened to me. I knew what I felt, what I saw, and what I heard, was so much bigger than myself, yet I felt desolate and alone.

In October 2013 during my state of misery, I called out to God in deep desperation and pain. I was tired of being depressed, tormented, confused. I longed for peace of mind and freedom. I longed for THIS to be over! In the midst of my tears and wailing, after days and days of praying, He finally answered me. In the gentlest whisper He said, "I kept you!" "You could have lost your mind, you could have

been gone, but I kept you."

"You could have lost your children, your home, everything, but I kept you."

"Satan wanted you, but My hand was on you!"

Immediately the weight of depression was lifted off me. I felt an intense joy, relief, freedom. I did not receive all the answers I was looking for, yet it was the clarity I needed to start my healing process and the restoration of my mind.

Even after this, I still had struggles. My depression was gone, I understood there was a battle for my sanity, but what was the bigger picture? As I constantly recounted the events that took place, I tried to interpret the events myself, and nothing really made sense. The LORD placed it on my heart to write a book about my mental breakdown, and I flat out said no. Months and months went by, as I continued to struggle with the understanding and embarrassment of why this happened to me, and now, He wants me to write a book about it?! I JUST DON'T GET!!!

Section Two: Their Side of the Story

TERRY

Thirteen months later, we found ourselves sitting around the same dining room table where I drank the Subway soup, now preparing for this interview. I can admit we were both a little nervous. We had not spoken up until two weeks prior to the interview.

Over the phone, she sounded so happy to hear from me, but when I saw her face to face, she smiled, but I could sense the uneasiness behind her smile. I was prepared for that. After all, our last encounter was very extreme, and she probably had doubts in her mind about me. We had literally just met before all this had taken place. I was very happy she would sit down with me and discuss the events. I did the best I could to make her feel at ease during the interview.

I began the interview by repeating what I could remember from the events taken place, what I had been through in the preceding months, and how everything led me to writing this book. I could tell there were a lot of similarities in our stories, as I told my version, and she nodded her head along. From the beginning at the hair salon to the phone call from seven-eleven, she remembered it more or less as I did. She told me we had just met that day! And I thought we had met days prior to this taking place! I allowed her to tell me the rest of the story from her point of view. When she was done, I asked, "At what point did you realize something was wrong with me?"

"When you went to the bathroom and wet yourself with your clothes on."

"What was going through your mind then?" "I didn't know what to think, I had just met you. I was afraid because I did not

44

know what to do. I knew something was wrong. What you did was not normal. After that I just wanted to take you home."

"Looking back, is there anything that you would have done differently?"

"Yes, I would have listened to you more. I thought to myself for days, what could I have done to help. I kind of faulted myself, but I did not know what to do. Sitting here with you now made me realize everything happened the way God intended for it to happen. If I would have intervened then, whatever God was doing in your life would not have ran its course and you wouldn't be sitting before me today." She went on to say, "I just didn't understand what was happening at the time, I was afraid."

IAN

I interviewed Ian at a park while our kids ran around and played on the swings and jungle gym. We had been communicating on and off, more off than on, but he agreed to do the interview when I asked him. He was very nervous as we sat across from each other on the park bench table. To try and ease his tension, I explained to him how the process was going to flow. I would tell what I remember, then he could share his story as far as he was comfortable sharing it. I pulled out my daughter's cell phone; her phone was more updated than mine, and hit the voice recording app in the menu. "Whoa! You didn't tell me that you were going to record this", Ian said and laughed.

I hit record and began the interview. I knew from the beginning this interview would be different, and a bit more difficult than the others. First reason being he had received a lot of the blame for why this happened to me from friends mutual and otherwise to my family. Secondly, because we had been in a relationship. However, I made up my mind I was not going to let none of that influence my perception or judgment on how I conducted this interview. He was there at the beginning when it all started, and I was more inquisitive to hear his side of the story over anything else, so I put all else out of my mind.

I began to tell the story beginning on Friday about the fast and our discussion about consecration. He expressed he remembered I had been fasting, but he could not recall the conversation we had earlier that day. Then he brought up the bedroom episode. He remembered it clearly. He remembered me piling the things on the bed and helping me separate them. I asked him if he had found that strange of me to do that, and he responded no. Then I asked him if he remembered lying on the floor, me praying over him, and the iron. As I mentioned it, it seemed as if it jumped back into his memory.

Ian: Yes, I remember that now, but I had forgotten about it.

Me: What was going through your mind then?

Ian: Honestly, I didn't think much of it. I have so much faith in your faith I didn't want to question it. I know how deep you were into seeking God. I know about your history in church, and how you've been following God since your mother had you all (my siblings and I) in church since kids.

Me: Looking back on the situation, was there anything you would have done differently?

Ian: No. I didn't know or understand what was going on at the time. I knew you had been fasting and praying and talking about how God had been speaking with you, but I never doubted your faith.

KAMILAH

I had been tracking down Kamilah for weeks, until I finally got a hold of her, and we set a date for her interview. She arrived at my house on a Friday, early afternoon. My girls were still in school, and we had a couple of hours to burn before they'd arrive home. She came in ready to do this interview, she was so enthusiastic. As she got settled in her chair, she made this comment, "I feel like I'm preparing for an interview for a major talk show. Like someone is going to come and do my make-up and hair!"

We both laughed. It really set the atmosphere for us to begin to recall and recount what happened fourteen months prior. Even with all this energy, she claimed to be tired. I offered her coffee, and then went into the kitchen to fix her a cup. We sat there for a couple hours just catching each other up on what was happening in each other's lives and speaking of God's mercy and His love for us even when we are at a moment in our life where we do not understand it enough to appreciate it. My girl's school bus pulled up, and I jumped up to open the door for them. That also reminded us that we had not even started the interview.

I began this interview like I had begun the previous two. I would start off by telling the events as I remembered, allow her to tell what she experienced, and then I would ask questions as we moved along. I began to paraphrase the beginning of the story and picked up where Terry and I pulled up to her apartment. I retold the events starting from me walking into her house, going straight to the bathroom, coming out, and beginning a conversation with her. She interjected, "When I heard the knock on my door, it was unexpected. When you said, 'It's Rumika', I thought it was odd for

48

you to be here, but no harm, and I didn't think too hard about it, because we were friends".

"I opened the door, and you walked right in and said you needed to use the bathroom. I closed the door, you went to the bathroom, I jumped back on my bed, and we were having a conversation through the bathroom door. When you came out, I noticed your demeanor had changed.".

She stated when I exited the bathroom, I was not the same person that went in.

"My friend Rumika went in that bathroom, but something else, I don't know what it was, came out!"

"Something triggered in my spirit", she said, "But I didn't adhere to it because it was you. Rumika, my friend, my sister in Christ, we encouraged each other in the Word, and I knew about your relationship with God."

We continued to tell our individual versions of the story and paused at times to allow it all to sink in as we realized how similarly different our stories were. We came up on the part of the story I mentioned earlier in the book; where I had asked her if there was something, she had to tell me. She revealed to me that was not the question I had asked her that day. Instead, she said I had asked her if she was sleeping with Ian! I screamed out, "What!"

She recalled me telling her, "God told me that!".

"The devil is a liar" she said.

"The God that I serve could not have told you that. I don't know who you are hearing from, but that's not God."

This is when she started to feel something strange was going on. She knew I knew she would never do anything of that nature to me, so she began to wonder where this was coming from. She told the rest of the story to me and how it really played out from that moment on. She told me something I had not remembered.

"Do you remember jumping up and down and screaming?".

"LET'S GO TO CHURCH! LET'S GO TO CHURCH! I WANT TO GO TO CHURCH!" I shook my head no.

"That's when I dropped to my knees," she said. Lifted my hands, and I screamed, "Jesus!" For surely I was face to face with a demon!"

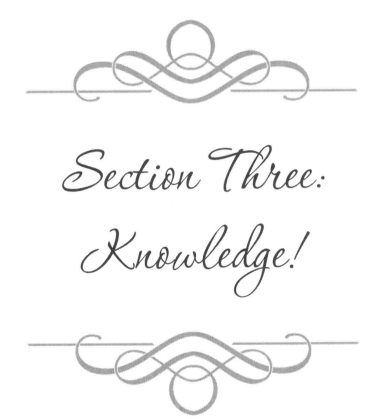

Section Three: Knowledge!

VICTORY

I was taken aback at how boldly she exclaimed, and she realized the demonic force at work within me. I knew something was not right with me, but I could not pinpoint it.

Again, I asked the question what is Spiritual Warfare, and why is it so important for us as Christ Followers to understand it? In his letter to the church of Ephesus, Paul writes in *Ephesians 6:12*

For our struggle is not against flesh and blood, but against the rulers, against the authorities, against the powers of this dark world and against the spiritual forces of evil in the heavenly realms. N.I.V.

Surely, we should have a degree of cognizance of such a topic. A faction of spiritual warfare is the internal battle taking place within the heart and the mind of an individual.

But there is another power within me that is at war with my mind. This power makes me a slave to the sin that is still within me.

Romans 7:23 N.L.T.

The sinful nature wants to do evil, which is just the opposite of what the spirit wants. And the spirit gives us desires that are opposite of what the sinful nature desires. These two forces are constantly fighting each other, so you are not free to carry out your good intentions.

Galatians 5:17, N.L.T.

The other faction of spiritual warfare is what takes place in the heavenly realms. We cannot see this war with our eyes, but we can be made aware of it through the eyes of the Holy Spirit. This is the war in which the Apostle Paul describes in Ephesians chapter six. It is through this war we experience the by-product of the evil taken place in the heavenly realms. The rulers of darkness, the authorities, the powers of the dark world, and the spiritual forces of evil manifest in the earth realm through vessels, i.e., people, us in the form of sin (anything that is in opposition to God).

The American Heritage Dictionary gives this definition of warfare: "An armed conflict between mast enemies, armies, or the like."

For the sake of understanding that you may obtain and sustain your victory, we will focus on the internal battle taking place over your heart and mind. The amazing concept of our fight is the hard part is done for us! Once you accepted Christ as your Lord and Savior; You know, reciting the Sinners Prayer:

"Dear God in heaven, I come to you in the name of Jesus. I acknowledge to You I am a sinner, and I am sorry for my sins and the life I have lived; I need your forgiveness. I believe your only begotten Son Jesus Christ shed His precious blood on the cross at Calvary and died for my sins, and I am now willing to turn from my sin.

You said in the Bible that if we confess the Lord our God and believe in our hearts that God raised Jesus from the dead, we shall be saved. Right now, I confess Jesus as my Lord. With my heart, I believe that God raised Jesus from the dead. This very moment I accept Jesus Christ as my own personal Savior and according to His Word, right now I am saved. Amen."

When you have done this, you vicariously have taken part in Jesus Christ's victory over the power of sin, which penalty is death, when He rose from the dead. Simply put. *Romans 6:23* Tells us: *The wages (consequences) of sin is death. K.J.V*

Death = Eternal separation from God.
Jesus' purpose, or His battle, was to ensure we did not spend eternity away from God in Hell, but with Him in Heaven. He did this by defeating death when He rose from the dead. To date, Jesus is alive in heaven sitting on the right hand of the Father!

Because He lives eternally, we too can live eternally.

You were dead because of your sins and because your sinful nature was not yet cut away. Then God made you alive with Christ, for He forgave all our sins. He cancelled the record of charges against you and took it by nailing it to the cross. In this way, He disarmed the spiritual rulers and authorities. He shamed them publicly by his victory over them on the cross.

Colossians 2:13-15 N.L.T.

That was Jesus' fight, and He won! We now must endure our own fight. While He may have died to destroy the power of sin, we must deal with the influence of sin. Hence, the internal battle over the heart and mind, as the Holy Spirit leads and teaches us how to shift our carnal desires to spiritual desires.

You might pose the question as to how did Christ disarm our enemies? The question is not how, rather what did he take back from them? The answer is Life and Freedom.

The saying goes, "Innocent until proven guilty." Well, that is not so in the Christian faith. Many believe if they are good people, through deeds and acts of kindness, they have obtained a free ticket into Heaven, part of God's eternity, unfortunately that is not so.

If you are susceptible to death, meaning, one day you WILL die, then you are guilty as charged of sin, rather, having a sinful nature. Remember the penalty for sin is separation from God.

The truth: we will all naturally one day leave this earth in death; this is evidence we are sinful beings by default. The Psalmist, King David, puts it as this,

For I was born a sinner, yes from the moment my mother conceived me.

Psalm 51:5 N.L.T.

The Amplified Bible reads:

I was brought forth in [a state of wickedness]; in my sin my mother conceived me [and from the beginning I, too was sinful].

In our faith the saying goes, "Guilty until proven innocent!". Then comes a chapter in God the Father's love story…

For God so loved the world He gave his ONLY Son. That whosoever continually believes in Him shall not perish but have everlasting LIFE!

John 3:16

The price for our lives was Christ's life, and He laid it down freely that we may be reconciled back to God for eternity. Therefore, a believer never dies, but transitions from the earthly life to a heavenly life, forever with God.

Now even though we are not dealing with the power of sin that leads to death, we still must live day by day, overcoming the influences of sin we are faced with in our personal life. No, we are not expected to live perfect lives, but daily we must choose to make decisions which will perfect the spirit of Christ within us.

Perfecting the spirit of Christ in you is an important process in practicing the faith of Christianity. When Father God deems the time fit for Jesus to return and take all believers in Him back to heaven, He is looking for faith and those who have inwardly conformed to His likeness. We are not expected to be as Jesus in

His divinity, but like Jesus in His humanity who was in full submission to the ways and will of God.

He [God] made Christ who knew no sin (His humanity) to be sin on our behalf (His divinity), so that in Him [Jesus] we would become the righteousness of God [that is, we would be made acceptable to Him and placed in a right relationship with Father God by His gracious lovingkindness].

2 Corinthians 5:21 A.M.P

Perfecting the Spirit of Christ in you comes from a relationship with Christ through the Holy Spirit. The Holy Spirit comes as a gift to all believers once they confess Christ as their Lord and Savior. You can think of Him as your God conscience teaching you God's way from "the corrupt man's" way of thinking. Also, He will convict and warn you when you stray away from the teachings and principles of Christ, giving you an understanding of your choices and leading you to make more Christ centered choices going forward.

We receive a deposit of the Holy Spirit that dwells within us, becomes distinguished in us more each day as we spend time in prayer and reading the Bible. He is the way by which God knows that we are His, and Christ's way of communicating with us, helping us, to live lives worthy of our calling. We will dive more into the role of the Holy Spirit in your life in a later chapter.

HIS VICTORY IS
YOUR VICTORY

When you visualize war, there are always two opposing sides, and the objective, no matter the reason for the war, is to obtain victory over the opposing side.

When we look in retrospect of kings and kingdoms, how they were established and functioned in times of war, we can get a better understanding of the authority and victory of our king, King Jesus and walk and operate under the same victory to obtain our own.

Let's start from the top: The Kingdom of God and the Kingdom of Heaven. The Kingdom of Heaven is God's operation. The Kingdom of God is the manifestation of that operation. As you read through the New Testament you will see these two terms. The Kingdom of Heaven where God the Father reigns is not affected by time, the Kingdom of God is.

Jesus prays in Matthew 6:10,

May Your kingdom come [Kingdom of God], May Your will be done ON earth, as it is in heaven [Kingdom of Heaven where past, present, and future are already established and coexist]. N.L.T.

Asked by the Pharisees when the Kingdom of God would come, He replied to them by saying,

The kingdom of God does not come with signs to be observed or with visible display, Nor will people say, Look! Here [it is]! or, See, [it is] there! For behold, the kingdom of God is within you [in your hearts] and among you [surrounding you].

Luke 17:20-21 AMPC

Here are the characteristics of the Kingdom of God where Jesus is Lord and King:

1. God's operation [ordained principles]
2. Ruled by time
3. Lives within us

The Kingdom of God and the Kingdom of Heaven are always in agreement. It is our will, your will that separates them. The Kingdom of God is activated by faith and is personified in the person of the Holy Spirit.

"If you love Me, keep My commandments [1.

God's Operation/Principles]. And I will pray the Father, and He will give you another Helper, that He may abide with you forever [2. Ruled by time] — the Spirit of truth, whom the world cannot receive, because it neither sees Him nor knows Him; but you know Him, for He dwells with you and will be in you [3. Lives within you!].

John 14: 15-17 N.K.J.V.

But when He, the Spirit of Truth, comes, He will guide you into all the truth [full and complete truth]. For He will not speak on His own initiative, but He will speak whatever He hears [from the Father—the message regarding the Son], and He will disclose to you what is to come [in the future].

John 16:13 A.M.P.

When Christ left and went back to the Kingdom of Heaven, unruled and not effected by time. The Holy Spirit came down from heaven/ released from the Kingdom of Heaven, to be the Kingdom of God in us so that we may become the sons of God, after the likeness of Jesus. The sons of God we are the light in a dark world because we carry the Truth of Jesus on the inside of us. We are by whom God, through His Spirit, manifest His works in time through us. Works of love, peace, truth, kindness, justice, and more [see Galatians 5:22-23] are all characteristics of God's kingdom. The kingdom of God is not simply for an outward expression. This is what Jesus wanted the religious leaders of His day to understand. The Kingdom of God is designed first to work inwardly, then outwardly like the old song, "Something on the inside, working on the outside, Oh what a change in my life!". He is designed to always agree with the agenda of the Kingdom of Heaven.

For there are three that bear witness in [the Kingdom of] heaven: The Father, the Word, and the Holy Spirit; and these three are one [agree in one].

1 John 5:7 N.K.J.V.

As Holy Spirit lives on the inside of you His duty is to put into place God's ordained principles in your life so that you my always walk I agreement with the agenda of the Kingdom of Heaven. His role is to continuously reveal to you the Truth that is in Jesus who is THE King in our Kingdom.

But this Man, after He had offered one sacrifice for sins forever, sat down at the right hand of God, from that time waiting till His enemies are made His footstool. For by one offering He has perfected forever those who are being sanctified. But the Holy Spirit also witnesses to us; for after He had said before, "This is the covenant that I will make with them after those days, says the Lord: I will put My laws into their hearts, and in their minds, I will write them...

Hebrews 10:12-16 N.K.J.V.

I just Don't Get it?

But in fact, Christ has been raised from the dead. He is the first of a great harvest of all who have died. So, you see, just as death came into the world through a man, now the resurrection from the dead has begun through another man. Just as everyone dies because we all belong to Adam, everyone who belongs to Christ will be given new life. But there is an order to this resurrection: Christ was raised as the first of the harvest; then all who belong to Christ will be raised when he comes back.

1 Corinthians 15:20-23 N.L.T.

So, what is the victory Christ Jesus our king passed down to us? The defeat of death! Remember death is the eternal separation from God. Sin is what separates us from God. Death is the penalty of sin. Jesus died so our sins may be forgiven. He rose from the dead, defeating its power, that eternal separation from God is not the portion of the steadfast believer.

Imagine, when the Kingdom of God is absolved by the Kingdom of Heaven, there is no time, only eternity. Can you imagine an eternity away from God? The books of Mathew, Luke, Revelation all describe this place as a place of torment where there will be a weeping and gnashing of teeth. Where we lost our authoritative dominance through the disobedience of Adam, we regained through faith, belief, trust, submission, and obedience to Christ. Because Jesus defeated death, since our lives are renewed and revived in Him, our sins are forgiven and we too, through Him have a chance to gain eternal life with God our Creator, and not eternal damnation away from Him.

A real king does not celebrate in true victory until all his people are safe and accounted for. If a king still has constituents still in bondage, then his victory is not absolute. Jesus did not die and was resurrected solely for Himself, He died for the sins of the world, giving everyone a chance to experience their own victory, which is eternal life with Him.

And I do this for the sake of the good news (the Gospel), in order that I may become a participator in it and share in its [blessings along with you]. Do you not know that in a race all the runners compete, but [only] one receives the prize? So, run [your race] that you may lay hold [of the prize] and make it yours!]

1 Corinthians 9:23-24 AMPC

UNDERSTANDING

You should now have a clearer understanding that Spiritual Warfare isn't something that takes place in the physical realm. What you are fighting against, you cannot see, touch, or hear. How are you supposed to go into combat against something that isn't tangible? It starts with one word: FAITH.

If you believe and have faith in God, the Holy Trinity: God the Father, God the Son, and God the Holy Spirit, you must also believe that Satan and his demonic affiliates are real as well. Like I once was, most Christians now are in denial about the influence of Satan and the powers he has in this earthly realm. They ignored it, and to a fault empowered him more through their ignorance.

Hosea 4:6 tells us, we perish for the lack of knowledge. As believers of the Christian faith, our knowledge, better yet our truths, come from the Holy Bible, God's written word brought forth by man under the influence of the Holy Spirit.

All scripture is God-breathed and is useful for teaching, rebuking, correcting, and training in righteousness. *2 Timothy 3:16, N.I.V.* Here's the thing, there are many arguments for and against the Bible. Its truths can be debated both ways. If you search hard and long enough you will find individuals and groups who will try to disprove the accuracy of the Bible's contents. In the same fashion, you can find individuals and groups with evidence who can justify that the Bible in its entirety is truth.

And without faith it is impossible to please God, because anyone who comes to Him must believe that He exists and that He rewards those who earnestly seek Him.

Hebrew 11:6 N.I.V.

Our reward for our faith towards the Bible as God's Word is revelation, insight, and understanding into what has been written. The foundation of your belief in Christ Jesus, and your promise into the Kingdom of Heaven is based on your continual belief and trust in God's written words as the absolute truth ready to reveal to you and in you!

Heaven and earth shall pass away, but my word shall not pass away!

Matthew 24:35; Luke 21:33 K.J.V.

Our belief that God's Word is the absolute truth does not negate the facts of science, medicine, or the history and culture of everyday life, which has a great deal of influence on who we are and how we function as the human race. However, the Bible offers a knowledge of information elevated above the knowledge of this world system and society. Th e only way to grasp the knowledge of the Bible is to have faith in it and become a seeker of its truth.

> Knowledge: "An acquaintance with facts, truths, or principles." (American Heritage Dictionary)

If you do not trust the validity of the information (or facts) that you have acquired, on any subject, how can you apply it so that you may reap the benefits of what you know? Answer: You cannot. To be transformed by any form of information you have acquired; you must have some level of confidence in its reliability.

Your dependency on the reliability of the knowledge presented to you allows you to make judgements and decisions according to the purpose and plan in which you have need for said information. You want and need the most reliable information and knowledge that you can get to equip you to make the right, or wisest decisions.

Wisdom: "Knowledge of what is true or right, coupled with judgment as to action; discernment, or insight." (A.H.D)

Wisdom is the principal thing; therefore, get wisdom: and with all thy getting, get understanding.

Proverbs 4:7 K.J.V.

Understanding: "(3) Superior power of discernment; enlightened intelligence." (A.H.D)

Understanding in the Christian faith is what ultimately sets us apart. We are not just consecrated against other religions or faiths because of our beliefs, but from the sociological and psychological patterns of the world system at large. Obtaining understanding based on Biblical principles makes us different, not better, than anyone else.

But you are a chosen generation, a royal priesthood, a holy nation, a peculiar people; that ye should shew forth the praises of Him who hath called you out of darkness into his marvelous light.

1 Peter 2:9 K.J.V.

The world at large needs salvation. We have made a choice to accept the only way to salvation, which is through Jesus Christ.

Trust in the Lord with all thine heart; and lean not unto thine own understanding. In all thy ways acknowledge Him, and He shall direct thy paths: Be not wise in thine own eyes fear the Lord and depart from evil.

Proverbs 3:5-7 K.J.V.

"My thoughts are nothing like your thoughts", says the Lord. "And my ways are far beyond anything you can imagine. For just as the heavens are higher than the earth, so my ways and thoughts higher than your thoughts."

Isaiah 55:8-9 N.L.T.

God's ways: His knowledge, His wisdom, His understanding, is so infinite, that our finite minds would literally dismantle itself if we tried to figure Him out.

Proverbs 3:5 exhorts us to trust in the knowledge, truths, and wisdom of God with all our hearts, and lean not to our own understanding. This means, do not try to figure it out! Many believers fall into error and deception because we use their own interpretation to the Word of God. Since the Word of God was brought forth through inspiration by Holy Spirit, then you will need Holy Spirit to translate, or explain it to you, enabling you to grasp the understanding of God, and not your own.

Verse six says, *"In all your ways acknowledge Him, and He will give you direction."* This whole salvation walk is to teach you how to transform from one mindset to another; one understanding to another; one way of thinking to another, which puts you in agreement and concordance with the Kingdom of Heaven. This happens by way of lessons taught to you and understanding brought to you by Holy Spirit, through the Word of God.

"But the Advocate, the Holy Spirit, whom the Father will send in my name, will teach you all things and remind you of everything I have said to you."

John 14:26 N.I.V.

Remember, the Holy Spirit is your God conscience. His job is to transform your way of thinking into Christ's way of thinking, by using the knowledge, understanding, and wisdom of God's Word. Through faith you have knowledge, wisdom, and understanding. Now you are committed to this fight, what is next?

KNOW YOUR
OPPONENT

Who is Satan? In *John 14:29*, Jesus calls Lucifer the prince of this world, which simplifies into the leader or ruler of this world. In *2 Corinthians 4:4*, the Apostle Paul calls Lucifer the god, or deity of this world, signifying he is worshipped and has worshippers. He is also known by other names throughout the scripture. In the New Testament, he is called the devil, which means slanderer or false accuser. In the Book of Matthew, Jesus and the Pharisees refer to him as the Beelzebub. Beelzebub can be translated to "Lord of the House" or "Lord of the Flies", known as the prince of the demons. Scripture also calls him the tempter, *1Thessalonians 3:5*, the wicked one, *Matthew 13:19*, accuser of the brethren, *Revelation 12:10*, and prince of the power of the air, *Ephesians 2:2*.

I want you to focus on two scriptural passages, for now, that you may gain a foundational understanding as to the history of Lucifer, and the authority and influence in which he now operates in. Read these two passages carefully. I suggest that you read them in different biblical versions, such as, the New Living Translation NLT, The Amplified Bible AMP, and the Message Bible MSG. *Ezekiel 28: 13-18* and *Isaiah 14:12-15*.

Ezekiel 28: 13-18

Thou hast been in Eden the garden of God; every precious stone was thy covering the sardius, topaz, and the diamond, the beryl, the onyx, and the jasper, the sapphire, the emerald, and the carbuncle, and gold: the workmanship of thy tabrets and of thy pipes was prepared in thee in the day thou wast created.

I just Don't Get it?

Thou art the anointed cherub that covereth; And I have set thee so: Thou wast on the holy mountain of God; Thou hast walked up and down in the midst of the stones of fire. Thou were perfect in thy ways from the day that thou wast created, till iniquity was found in thee. By the multitude of thy merchandise they have filled the midst of thee with violence, and thou hath sinned: Therefore, I will cast thee as profane out of the mountain of God: And I will destroy thee, O covering cherub, From the midst of the stones of fire.

Thine heart was lifted up because of thy beauty, Thou hast corrupted thy wisdom by reason of thy brightness: I will cast thee to the ground, I will lay thee before kings, that they may behold thee. Thou hast defiled thy sanctuaries by the multitude of thine iniquities by the iniquity of thy traffick; Therefore, I will bring forth a fire from the midst of thee, It shall devour thee, And it will bring thee to ashes upon the earth in the sight of all them that behold thee.

K.J.V Isaiah 14: 12-15

How art thou fallen from heaven, O Lucifer, son of the morning! How art thou cut down from the ground, which didst weaken the nations! thou hast said in thine heart, I will ascend into heaven, I will exalt my throne above the stars of God: I will sit also upon the mount of the congregation, In the sides of the north: I will ascend above the heights of the clouds; I will be like the Most High. Yet thou shalt be brought down to hell, to the sides of the pit. K.J.V

It is the understanding and the belief of the Christian faith that God, Elohim, created everything and everyone in six days then on the seventh day He rested. Since God created everything within the parameter of six days, this tells us that Lucifer was created in this time frame as well, along with all of creation.

For through Him [Jesus] God created everything in the heavenly realms and on the earth. He made the things we can see, and things we can't see, such as thrones, kingdoms, rulers, and authorities in the unseen world.

Colossians 1:16 N.L.T.

When we dissect the scriptural text of Ezekiel the twenty-eighth chapter, verses thirteen through eighteen, we see the beauty in which Lucifer was created. The text tells us he was composed of every precious stone; diamonds and rubies, sapphires, topaz, the onyx, emeralds, and set in the finest gold! Not only that, but in him was placed the sound of a vast array of musical instruments. His very movement and posture created melodies unto God. He was perfect in his ways, conduct, and behavior, until the day that iniquity entered his heart.

Iniquity is the continuous act of sin. Sin is to miss the mark (disobedience), the mark (standard of God's Righteousness). Through the abundance of your commerce [spiritual or intellectual interchange], you were internally filled with violence and you sinned, *Ezekiel 28:16, A.M.P.*

For you said to yourself, "I will ascend to heaven and set my throne above God's stars... I will climb to the highest heavens and be like the Most High."

Isaiah 14: 13a, 14 N.L.T.

Lucifer concocted a plan in his heart. He would exalt himself as the highest, most important, revered being, by way of revolt against God, Elohim, the Creator. The seventeenth verse of the twenty-eighth chapter of Ezekiel, Lucifer reasoned that he deserved to be in the position as God because of his beauty, his outward appearance and his talents.

Lucifer was an anointed cherub, or angel of the highest class. The only one that was allowed onto the mountain, or the level in the heavens where God would manifest certain characteristics of His glory. There is a belief floating around the Body of Christ that it was Lucifer's JOB to worship God, and that is very far from the truth. A job would denote that he had earned the right through his own qualifications to obtain that position. He did not work for

God; he was created by God for God's purpose. His purpose was to be a reflection of God amongst the host of the heavens.

We see a demonstration of this in the life of Moses. Exodus the thirty-fourth chapter, tells of a story of Moses meeting with God face to face. When he would return to the Israelite camp his face radiated with light, which was evidence of God's glory and presence. This was a sign and evidence to Moses' fellow brethren, not only was he in the presence of God, but he received insight into God and from God.

Yes, indeed Lucifer was beautiful. The greatest of stones were his covering. However, it was only in the presence of God, he could see how beautiful he was. His beauty had nothing to do with his outward appearance, but everything to do with who he was a reflection of. You cannot see the true beauty of any precious stone, unless light permeates it.

God is light, and there is no darkness in Him at all!

1 John 1:5 K.J.V.

When Lucifer, which means light bearer or bearer of light, would go before the presence of God, God exposed Lucifer to a form of His glory, light! The light from God would permeate every fiber of his being giving off a spectacular display of colors into the atmosphere of the heavens. He was created to be the bearer of God's light, and not the light itself. By design, the hosts of heaven would worship God from the knowledge or information Lucifer received in this ordained place.

The text from Ezekiel tells us the wisdom and knowledge he gained about God was corrupted and perverted by vanity. He took his heart and focus from God and created his own agenda.

He drew away a number of the angels through knowledge. Scripture says, through Lucifer's iniquity of trafficking information he defiled the hosts of heavens, and because of this, he lost his position as the anointed cherub, and his place in heaven. His demise was not in the world view that he is simply evil — His demise was found in the choice that he made in the will of his own heart. His iniquity was not a mere thought, but he carefully devised a plan to go against the order in which the all-knowing God orchestrated as his purpose and his lot to erect a kingdom and a throne above the Most High God, declaring war on God, moving from and instrument of worship, to the object of worship. For this reason, God cast him from the midst of the heavens, and he received the sentence of his judgement that day.

The prince of this world is already judged.

John 16: 11 K.J.V.

Knowing your opponent is half the strategy. Being aware of the history of your opponent is a strategy used in almost every competitive sport. Teams would study their opposition, watch their video footages, paying attention to key players, games tactics, and techniques. The same goes for us as believers. We must know and understand how our enemy Lucifer, better known as Satan or the Devil, moves and operates, so we may not be caught off guard, or fall victim to his schemes.

Lest Satan should gain the advantage over us; for we are not ignorant of his devices.

2 Corinthians 2:11 N.K.J.V.

71

IT'S ALL GOOD
IN LOVE AND
HOLINESS

Whenever God looked upon a nation, a people, He looked upon it as a woman. We can see this in the Book of Isaiah 54th chapter verses 1-6. Also, in the Book of Revelation the 19th and 20th chapter the writer refers to the body of believers as the bride of Christ. This is done to depict a love relationship between God and those whom He has called and chosen as His own. The purpose of this as with any relationship goes far beyond the emotions and feelings of love, but to come together in intimacy as to produce an offspring.

You see what we experience in nature, through love and marriage when the husband and wife come together and produce a baby, a child they themselves love and nurture and care for it while it grows. This is the same for us as believers, but this is done for us and with us not in the natural, but in the spiritual. We grow in a loving and close relationship with God, and He produces in us a new heart and a new mind.

God knows each and every one of us. So much so that He knows the number of hairs upon your head, my head, your mother's head, my mother's head, my father's head, your father's head, etc. etc. etc. get it? He knows each of us intricately, and He wants you to know Him intimately that He may produce in you and through you godly characteristics and spiritual fruit leading you into the purpose and plan He has for your life.

Before you engage in any relationship, it is important that you understand the identity and character of the person you are getting involved with. Understanding also, who you are and the character you yourself possess. Let me introduce you to a Man that loves you regardless of your color, creed, your past mistakes, or your present situation.

For I am persuaded, that neither death, nor life, or angels, nor principalities, nor powers, nor things to come, nor height, nor depth, nor any other creature, shall be able to separate you from the Love of God, which is in Christ Jesus our Lord.

Romans 8:38-39 K.J.V.

GOD IS HOLY!

No one is Holy like the Lord! Th ere is none besides you; there is no rock like our God. 1 Samuel 2:2 N.L.T.

And He expects us to be Holy as well!

You must be Holy, for I Am Holy!

1 Peter 1:16 N.L.T.

God's holiness is His goodness.

God's definition of good is far different than your understanding of what good is. In the Book of Mark, a rich man refers to Jesus as good. Jesus' response to him was, "Why do you call me good? For there is only one that is good, and that one person is God!" Why would Jesus say only God is good? Does that mean we are all bad? No, of course not! In the Book of Genesis, aft er God saw they created man, he called His creation very good. Jesus has the understanding there is no one as pure in essence but

73

God. God's pureness is what sets Him apart from all kinds. Th is pureness of who He is, is what makes Him Holy.

In order to understand what holiness is, you have to relinquish your definition of good. You might say someone's acts of kindness or their lack of evil doing is what qualifies a person to be good. Then I'll refute, "What is good? What is evil? And by whose standard?". We may have some collective lists of what we consider to be bad vs. good, but none of our standards are even close to the standard and understanding of God's ways and thoughts.

"My thoughts are nothing like your thoughts," says the Lord. "And my ways are far beyond anything you could imagine. For just as the heavens are higher than the earth, so ways are higher than your ways and my thoughts higher than your thoughts."

Isaiah 55:8-9 N.L.T.

One Sunday morning during corporate worship, I went up to the altar as an act of reverence toward God. As I was there, I was ushered deeper into the presence of God and I began to weep. The Lord our God says this to me, "Rumika, I am Holy.". Then He waits, and says, "You don't even deserve to be in My presence!". In utter shock, my cry turned into a strong uncontrollable weeping as I got a glimpse of God's holiness (Which I can't explain if I tried), and in a split second through a vision, I was forcibly pulled away from Him like to repelling magnets in opposite directions. It seemed as if there were eternities between us. I stood there and cried, and cried, and cried, because I loved God and I wanted to be near Him, in His presence. The knowledge of being separated from Him, lefty me in despair, feeling rejected, and without hope. Just when I had reached the height of those feelings, He said to me, "It is my love that allows Me to come near unto you!". Immediately the distance closed between us because of love. I dropped to my knees. From that moment my worship and my respect for who God is has never been the same.

And you must love the lord your God with all your heart, all your soul, and all your strength.

Deuteronomy 6:5 N.L.T.

Most of our issues with love are not giving it but receiving it! It is easy for us to disperse love, but when it comes to receiving it, we run it through a dozen checkpoints like a TSA agent at an airport to verify its validity. We trust our hearts to love but do not trust others to love us. Our concept of love has either one or both of these flaws: 1). It's one sided, or 2). It's not mutual between partners.

One sided love is demand love, with no real commitment or loyalty. Demanding love is a selfish love. This person only cares about what you can do for them. If you cannot meet their need for things and/or attention, then you do not love them. They always come first, but never give out and if they do it is for their benefit not yours.

Love that is not mutual flows like this: You have two individuals who have two separate concepts of what love is and how it is supposed to portray itself. One mate loves the other how they "think" that person should be loved, and because "I Love You this way", I expect "You to Love Me that way" without ever communicating what each individual need, wants, and is willing to accept. What happens here is a cycle of broken communication and misunderstandings that never interprets one person's heart toward the other. This love is dangerous because it most often stems from a physical or emotional attraction that is driven by infatuation. Because this person feeds a certain desire in the mind of your emotions, you force yourself to be with this person even though you both have a different concept of love, relationship, and intimacy. I believe this is the category where Ian and I fell into.

In order for you to love God with all of your heart, soul, mind, and strength and receive His love, you must first find out what love is. Rather who love is.

Beloved, let us love one another: For love is of God; and everyone that loveth is born of God, and knoweth God. He that loveth not knoweth not God; for God is love.

1 John 4:7-8 K.J.V.

1 Corinthians 13 describes the character of love as this,

Love is patient. Love is kind. Love is not jealous or boastful or proud or rude. It does not demand its own way. It is not irritable (overly sensitive or easily angered), and it keeps no record of being wronged. It does not rejoice about injustice but rejoices when truth wins out. Love never gives up, never loses faith, is always hopeful, and endures through every circumstance.

Since 1 John 4 tells us that God is love. Wherefore God is love, He is the standard of love. He is the standard of patience. He is the standard of kindness. He teaches you not to be jealous, boastful, proud or rude, according to His standard. He is not selfish, runs by His emotions, easily angered, or keeps a record of wrong. Neither does He rejoice when injustice happens, for He is the standard of justice and judgement. He'll never give up. He wants you to never lose faith, He is hope, and He endures through all. God is the standard in the actions of love. Just as His ways and thoughts are far different than your own, so is His love (He is) far different than what we believe love (and Him) to be.

God is more patient than He is portrayed. He is kinder than He is portrayed. He is not as demanding as we and others make Him.

He is not selfish; He doesn't spend His days mad thinking of ways to destroy mankind. He won't give up or walk away from you so easily. Many of us have a misconstrued concept of love far from its truth. This is evident in our world and society that praise self-righteousness, self-sufficiency and independence, non- committal or short- term relationships and agreements, and vindictive thought pattern and belief systems when it comes to relationships across every spectrum of social, business, religious, intimate, and personal interaction. I believe this pattern of thought stems from a misappropriation of love, honor, and respect. We as believers in Christ cannot operate on this world and societal view of love which pushes and teaches an agenda of tolerance in a hope to discover God's love in the process. You cannot think like the world does and hope to discover God.

The world system of love is based on passions and emotions: what feels good, and what makes you feel good. If anything is contrary to any of these notions, that which is contrary, is not love. The world view of love teaches comfortability. What is familiar to you. These, more times than often, turn out to be devastating circumstances for they are proven not to be safe or healthy physically, mentally, emotionally, or socially. When we talk about love, we need to get to the essence of its nature. It's like what we discussed with holiness: It's the pureness of God's essence and nothing on earth, under it, or in the heavens can compare to it, this is why He is God. Love is the same way. It has an essence, a character, a validity, a standard. Since God is Love, Love [God] cannot be taught nor explained to you, He can only be revealed through knowing Him! As a believer of Christ, you are never called to love God through your emotions.

Love the Lord your God and keep His requirements, His decrees, His laws, and commands always.

> *Deuteronomy 11:1 N.I.V.*

If you love me, keep my commandments.

> *John 14:15 K.J.V.*

Your love for God is displayed through acts of obedience. Love professed between you and God is not to be expressed solely as an emotion, but as actions to be shown. The Type A Soldier commits themselves to their emotions and is destroyed or conquered in battle. I want you to understand this: God gave you your emotions as a way to communicate with Him and other individuals. However, you are not to be controlled and led astray merely by your emotions but use them as a means to convey what you feel in order to arrive at a solution that produces an action.

In return, God's love is His actions towards you. These actions turn into interactions which produce a sense of belonging. A connection between you and God. It's a bond of affections that are not dependent upon emotions, but as you share in one another's lives, your emotions depict how you feel towards Him, and you will begin to understand how He feels about you. He wants to reveal His heart to you and reveal what's in your heart to you.

Jeremiah 17:9 says, *"The heart is deceitful and desperately wicked: who can know it?".*

The purpose of revealing what's in your heart, is first and foremost Truth. God will always be honest with you and desires you to be honest with Him. Secondly, He shows you what is in your heart to reveal to you the fallacies of your standard of truth and goodness. As you accept the truth of your erroneous standard you can be led to a lifestyle of mental, emotional, spiritual freedom, and obedience in Christ.

Then Jesus said to those Jews [you] which believed in Him, If you continue in my word, then you are my disciples [followers] indeed: And you shall know the truth, and the truth shall make you free.

John 8:31-32 K.J.V.

The secret things belong unto the Lord or God: but those things which are revealed belong into us and our children forever, that we may do all the words of this law.

Deuteronomy 29:29 K.J.V.

Like all relationships, your relationship with God will take work. God has work to do [*Philippians 1:6*], and you have work to do [*John 14:15* and *2 Timothy 2:15*]. Action. When you respond to His actions, love, in the proper manner, you can begin to understand the truth behind your purpose and existence. See yourself as a tree which started out as a seed. Naturally seeds need water to grow into whatever they are purposed for. Rose seeds will grow into roses, orange seeds into oranges, and so forth. Despite what the world system says, the creator desires a relationship with His creation. When you accepted Christ as your Lord and Savior, the seed of Christ was placed in you and God marked you as His own through the Holy Spirit, for the purpose of producing in you a Christ-like character and mindset.

It is not God's love which must be proven for you, but your love for Him. His love nor His faithfulness or His commitment to you ever sways or changes. He is the same yesterday, today, and forever more. He is the beginning of everything, and the ending of everything. Everything exists within Him. He does not ever change, neither does His standards nor His love. It is your heart that must

79

be tested, tried, healed, and conformed to match the understanding of His commitment to you. You must learn love. Then, learn how to love, first God, then others. You must get past the concept of love always feeling good. Love when it is done in the Spirit of Truth, cuts, it hurts, and at times, depending on what it reveals, is painful and hard to accept; but it always breeds life, truth and growth.

You yourself have a purpose, and the fullness of that purpose is birthed out through the watering of God's love upon your heart. This is not a touchy feely type of love, but a love that is strong and powerful to change and conform your heart from the nature it was birthed into. Your sin nature.

Section Four:

Guard Your Mind

KNOW HIS TACTICS: WARRIOR A, B, OR C

Terry, Ian, and Kamilah, represent three different types of warriors in Spiritual Warfare. I am so grateful that these three brave souls agreed to be a part of this book, and I am not trying to demoralize them in any way. In fact, all of us fall into one or more of these categories, or were once in one or more of these categories. Through my personal experiences shared with you in the first part of this book, I would like to introduce to you these three types of behaviors, which I will call warriors to denote specific characteristics and mindsets to show, teach and help us all in Spiritual Warfare.

Remember this is a war over your soul, affection, and love. Th e decisions you make on a daily basis will either empower you and draw you closer to eternal life with God or dissuade or seduce you away from the truth leading to eternal separation from the Lord. Each one of the following types of warrior is a Christ Follower. Placed on the battlefield, live in action, each one of us will exemplify one or more of these characteristics.

WARRIOR:
TYPE A

Type A Warrior: Contemplates or Makes Decisions Through Emotions

Terry openly admitted to me that she was afraid. Fear had overtaken her, and it paralyzed her into a position where she did not know how to respond. She just wanted to get me home, and away from her. The situation honestly snuck up on her, she was caught off guard and unprepared to handle it. Well, isn't that the same way that Satan works?

1 Peter 5:8 tells us

Be alert and of sober mind. Your enemy the devil prowls around like a roaring lion looking for someone to devour. N.I.V.

What are some of the emotions that you are operating in that is causing you to be paralyzed unable to react, or to respond erroneously? Is it doubt, anxiety, stress, frustration, anger, rage, jealousy, loneliness, or hurt? You've been in one situation or another, where someone has offended you, or pushed your buttons the wrong way and you reacted. You did not consider the outcome; you simply reacted and had to deal with the consequences of your actions afterward. Why? Because you got caught up in your emotions, and what you were feeling at the time. You did not take a moment to think before you reacted, and probably found yourself in a deeper mess and/or ended up with your foot in your mouth.

When you react in your emotions, your judgment is foggy, and you're thinking process has become irrational, and not Biblical. The thoughts you are having may seem right, but they are misconstrued, and unreliable. Amid Spiritual Warfare, any action that you take based on your emotions, can be detrimental to you in battle.

TACTIC #1 SABTOGE

We have already established that Spiritual Warfare deals with forces that are real; however, we cannot see them or touch them unless they are manifested. As you continue to read, especially as it pertains to that of the spirit, do not try to understand it with your natural intellect. Instead, ask God for understanding, and allow what has been written through the Holy Spirit to bear witness to your heart and mind. Read by faith!

Satan's ultimate goal is to sabotage your relationship with God; your love and your heart towards Him. One of the main entry ways Satan uses to gain control of your heart is to plant a seed in your mind through your thoughts. If Satan can produce a thought in your mind, he can produce an emotion. If he can produce an emotion, then he can produce an action.

Being a believer, especially a new believer, the Word of God [Bible], and a prayer life is imperative and should become distinctive to your life. I cannot stress enough how vital these two components are to your survival on earth as a citizen in God's Kingdom, in warfare, and in preparation to meet Jesus on that day. Your prayer life makes you sensitive to the Spirit and voice of God. The more you pray, the more aware and sensitive you will become about yourself [actions and thoughts], and the environment around you, seen and unseen, as well as becoming more sensitive to the leading and the voice of the Holy Ghost.

Prayer is not merely just talking to God as some may say. Yes, God loves it when we talk to Him! He welcomes conversations and topics that plague our heart and mind. However, when we pray, this takes on a different demeanor and posture. Our conversations with God are more casual, with prayer comes a reverence and a respect which causes you to posture yourself as the lesser being petitioning the Most Supreme Being to move on your behalf. Prayer is a tool. It can also yield itself as a weapon in the spiritual realm IF you know how to use it properly.

Teach us how to pray! Luke 11:1

Jesus in His time on earth was a bad man, bad as in He became unprecedented and performed such miracles, signs, and wonders. Even in oration He left many perplexed asking of Him, "What manner of man is this?". Jesus had a secret weapon, and after much observation the disciples figured it out, Prayer. Prayer is an embodiment of faith, scripture, patience, and trust. It is through proper application of prayer can we dissect through the spiritual realm and download the Lord's blueprint for strategy and victory.

Recently, while lying down one evening, God took me into an open vision. At first glance there was pitch darkness. Then appeared a being, who I understood in this vision to be Satan, or as he was, Lucifer. I watched as he flew up and up and up deeper into the utter darkness. Then he came to a stop and began simply waiting. Every now and again he would move to the left or move to the right, but never from the vicinity in which he originally stopped. As I pondered as to reason or the explanation of what I was seeing, Holy Spirit began to minister to me. Even at one point in time Satan, before he was expelled from heaven, had to find His way into the presence of G_D. He needed faith, trust, and the guidance of Holy Spirit to locate G_D's presence and place of habitation. As you have read earlier, Satan was the only anointed cherub, the only one who was allowed to climb to the most sacred place of G_D where He would reveal Himself in His glory. Satan had the honor of making that trip every single day, with the

85

responsibility of returning to the host of heaven and leading them into worship of the Most Holy God. In that moment I knew and understood why Jesus relished Himself in prayer, and why Satan fights the believer so much in their prayer life and in our faith.

And they overcame him by the blood of the Lamb and by the word of their testimony, and they did not love their lives to the death. Therefore rejoice, O heavens, and you who dwell in them! Woe to the inhabitants of the earth and the sea! For the devil has come down to you, having great wrath, because he knows that he has a short time.

Revelations 12:11-13 N.K.J.V.

The Word of our testimony is Prayer. Prayer is about stealing away from the cares of this world, finding a moment of solitude, quietness, where you can clear your mind and focus on one thing, connecting to the presence of God so He can reveal Himself to You. Jesus would steal away for hours at a time in prayer and in communion with the Father. Many believers are unsuccessful in their walk because of a weak and undisciplined prayer life. The enemy knows the most dangerous person on earth is one who sacrifices all to get into the Presence of God in the posture of prayer. In the presence of God mysteries are revealed, secrets are downloaded, any man who finds themselves in that place cultivate a oneness with God where they become His glory carriers on earth having the necessary understanding, wisdom, knowledge, and tools to effectively speak and intercede on the behalf of themselves and many others.

So, what does Satan do, everything he can to dissuade you from the depths and the power of prayer. Prayer should be indispensable in the life of a believer. Sad to say I observed over the years the propensity of believers to substitute praying with devotionals, scripture readings, conferences, and the like. While all these are great means in developing the Spirit of Christ in a believer, they should not be taking the place of a cultivated and disciplined prayer life. Prayer takes time. If you have not already, you should be setting time aside from your day, preferably in the morning to seek the Lord for the day ahead. When you do as Lucifer did, separate yourself, yield yourself to the voice of the Holy Spirit by faith, when you get to that place of stillness, and quietness, be patient, and trust that the LORD will reveal Himself to you giving you clarity and understanding when and where you need it. Situations and circumstances will begin t shift in your favor.

As a part of the Body of Christ, you can only find out what is required of you in life through prayer and by taking time to read and study God's story and history with mankind, the Bible. In it you will discover the power, the voice, and the heart of God Elohim, your Creator. He will teach you, through His Spirit and Power, His righteousness, His dos and don'ts with understanding and clarity. The consistency of prayer will give you a greater level of sensitivity to hearing God's response to your prayers and in your conversations. Every time you pick up the Bible, before you read, you should pray, "Spirit of God teaches me about God today. Give me understanding in and through His Word today. Teach me about His will, instructions, and directions for my life. Amen!" It is that simple. The depth of revelation of the Word of God will come in time with consistency and discipline.

It can be a challenge to begin a habit of daily Bible reading and prayer. I want to encourage you to start somewhere. Start with reading a scripture a day, a chapter a day. Start with five minutes of prayer, and increase your time daily, weekly, and as you grow. Meditate on the Word of God, read it over and over for a few days, even a week. Get it into your mind and heart. You must train your mind and heart, your spiritual appetite, to desire godly things. It is like starting a new diet. It is hard at first to deal with the changes and the old cravings you still have, but you must push past those feelings, and build a discipline that will change your life.

Biblical scripture is designed to give you insight into the mind, heart, and will of God. The Bible has great depth, and it is vast, you will never come into the full knowledge and mind of God, but you can strive every day to know Him truly. One day at a time! Do not overload yourself, do not stress yourself, and most importantly do not beat yourself up. This is a process of conformation. When a very sick person goes to a surgeon, the surgeon never performs multiple surgeries at one time. It will kill the patient. Instead, the surgeon performs one surgery at a time, allowing time for recuperation and healing, physically, emotionally, and mentally before the patient goes under again.

Lastly, concerning prayer, the Word, and the will of God — You cannot pray the will of God without the Word of God. You can have conversations with God all day, and at any time. When it comes to prayer, in order to become more and more effective in seeing results and aligning your will with the will of Kingdom of God inside of you, and, the Kingdom of Heaven, you must pray the Word concerning that which you are facing. The Word of God sets precedence to what is permitted and not permitted, legal vs. illegal. Remember Jesus prayed, "Let your will be done on earth as it is in heaven. There are sovereign and dominant laws established by God to rule both heaven and earth. Heaven is without sin, and therefore in perfect agreement to God's laws. Because of sin on earth, the domain of man, is no longer under direct simultaneous agreement. That agreement must be released into the earth realm through prayer by what is established as legal in heaven.

You gain understanding as to what the LORD considers legal or illegal through His written Word and revelation. When you pray, you pray with that understanding, allowing the work and will of God to be done in your life and on your behalf.

God's written Word is made for this very reason, to give you understanding about who He is, who you are, what you were created for, to make you aware of and to stand against the tactics of Satan. Through prayer, you are made aware and sensitive to the plots, and schemes of the devil. *John 10:10* tells you that, "*Satan, [the thief] comes to steal, kill, and destroy.* Therefore, when tested of the devil, Christ on all three occasions replied It Is Written, or This is legal. Satan knows the Word/ Laws of God as well. He will use a perverted version of God's Word to try and deceive you, so you must make time I your daily schedule to get acquainted with it. Satan did quote a portion of Psalms 91 to Jesus, but Jesus understood the will and law of God and did not settle for the words that came out of Satan's mouth. He knew Satan's ultimate motive, and that was to turn Him against God by getting Him to disobey Him. For this reason, it is very important for you to know and understand the Word of God and its legality as you pray.

<u>In Spirit and In Truth</u>

But of the tree of the knowledge of good and evil, thou shalt not eat of it: for in the day that thou eatest thereof thou shalt surely die.

Genesis 2:17 K.J.V.

Who you are is a spirit, you live in a body, and you have a soul? Your spirit is the essence of who you truly are. It is purposed as your divinity being one with God. You have a soul, which is your mind (your thoughts), will (what you are empowered to do), and emotions (feelings). Both your soul and your spirit were created to always be in alignment and agreement with God's heart and mind, being totally submitted to Him. However, this submission is not the form of submission you are familiar with today, this submission represented a form of coexisting. In the beginning man coexisted with God! But all this changed when Adam listened to the voice of His wife and disobeyed God. This act of disobedience shifted the dynamic of mankind inwardly as the Spirit of God broke agreement within us relinquishing us of our divinity leaving us without the inherent power of God. Picture Jesus at the peak of His glory before He left earth… That was Adam and Eve. That should have been us through them. That is us and will become us through Christ Jesus. Amen!

Because Adam and Eve were the first of God's creation their lineage would be a product of who they are in spirit, soul, and body. An apple seed will not produce oranges, it will produce apples. Adam and Eve, made after the image and likeness of God, were given permission in Genesis to be fruitful and multiply creating sons and daughters in their image and likeness, hence sons and daughters after the image and likeness of God. Unfortunately, as history would tell it, it did not go accordingly. Adam sinned against God by hearkening to the voice of another consequently disobeying Him.

This act of disobedience severed the internal spiritual connection mankind possess naturally with God, creating natural flow of brokenness and a severing of divine connection from God. Mankind lost his divinity through sin. We could no longer produce after the pure image and likeness of God, based on His standard and level of goodness and holiness; now any child produced would be born under the nature of sin and not the divine nature of God. The forfeiture of our divine nature is what God considers death.

<u>My Soul Shall Make Its Boast in the LORD</u>

Genesis 2:7 says

And the Lord formed man of the dust of the ground and breathed into his nostrils the breath of Life; and man became a living soul.

The breath of God awakened the soul of man. The awakening of our soul is what enables and activates the choices we make in our mind, through our will, and with our emotions. Pre-sin, because of our coexistence and relationship with and to God, our choices were always in alignment with His. God never demanded our choice; He required our obedience. He wanted and still wants us to choose Him; and we enjoyed that level of dependency and submission outside of sin. We lost our divinity, kept our life, and now we live according to our own mind/thoughts will, emotions, your soul. The relinquishing of our divinity, the inherent power of God, which was the Spirit of God, which is the Holy Spirit left us leaving us to discern what is good vs. what is evil. The problem with this is we filter knowledge through our own will, mind, and emotions. Every people, tribe, nation, religion, culture, etc. has their own standard of what is good or evil leaving us with varying degrees of both. Who is correct? No one but God.

We, being formed from that which was natural could only be anchored with God through His divine presence in us. It was our gift. It was our reminder here on earth that we were not alone. When we lost that we became lesser beings spiritually from our original design, and God's intent at that time for our lives. We are still spirit, but this spirit has no power. Yet it seeks for the knowledge of God with no clear direction or pathway to obtain it. Hence the birthing, the brooding, and the search to acquire all types of knowledge, but there is only one knowledge that could save your soul. Your spirit will submit to whatever you feed it or the lack thereof.

This absence of divinity and the empowering of the soul is what sets mankind on the path of eternal separation from God based on misinterpretations of degrees of knowledge. But then came Jesus!

When you received Jesus Christ as your Lord and Savior, you receive a second deposit of God's breath into your being. This second breath brings you from a place of spiritual death to spiritual life. The second breath is a redeposit of Holy Spirit in you. No, you are not the fullness of your divine self again, but you are now plugged into your divine source and must train and nurture your spirit how to coexist with God again. Hence the discipline in prayer, studying and reading the Word, and fasting (which we'll cover later) enabling your life, spirit, to submit to the life/spirit of Holy Ghost.

The Spirit of God, who raised Jesus from the dead, lives in you. And just as God raised Christ Jesus from the dead, He will give life to your mortal bodies by this same Spirit living within you.

Romans 8:11 N.L.T.

Remember I said that God's love produces in you a Christ-like character and mind. He does this through Holy Spirit and His power. The Holy Spirit carries the seed, the spiritual genetic makeup of God. The gene code of your divinity.

The fight of your life is to bring your whole self back into alignment with the will and order of God. This is the basics of Spiritual Warfare. Paul says it like this:

For the flesh desires what is contrary to the Spirit, and Spirit what is contrary to the flesh. They are in conflict with each other, so that you are not to do whatever you want [the desires of the Spirit of God in you].

Galatians 5:17 N.I.V.

Your soulish nature is your desire, your will, mind, and emotion. Your soul is a gift from God. All of you is a gift from God. Desires are things that you crave, want, and long for. These desires shape who you are and who you can become. All of these

92

things are influenced by your natural senses: what you hear, what you see, what you touch or what touches you, what you taste, and what you smell. Your senses feed your emotions which feed your thoughts, which feed your actions. Your soulish nature, your natural senses, and your emotions make up your flesh. The part of you that engages with the natural world. The flesh can have a negative connotation in relation to the spirit because of the sin passed down to you from Adam. This nature will always desire what is contrary to good, to God.. When you die your spirit/breath goes back to God and your soul/flesh, which is the sum of choices you made in your body/flesh. are judged for your deeds. For your deeds to be approved by God, remember, His standards of Holiness, you must train your soul to resubmit to your divine nature, God's Spirit in you. So, on one end you're training your spirit how to coexist with God again, and on the other end you're training your flesh to obey your spirit.

Being confident of this very thing, that He which began a good work in you will perform until the day of Jesus Christ!

Philippians 1:6 K.J.V.

This starts with a process of renewing your mind and your spirit daily. Remember, your spirit will submit to whatever you feed it, and so will your mind. The Bible needs to become your best friend. God spoke through man and they wrote as they were inspired by His Holy Spirit. We can get into all the logistics of how through the Bible was copied down through the ages and the mistakes that may or not be there. I believe that even if there were mistakes God has a way of revealing Himself through those mistakes so that this Word, the Bible represents His absolute Truth. God is infallible in all He does. I will admit being at one time very premature in spirit the Word, the Bible, did not make sense to me as a whole. But the

93

more I read it, and studied it, prayed, walked in obedience and truth through the years, God reveled His mysteries to me by joining together what was hidden and what is written.

The renewing of your mind and spirit takes place when you swap out old belief systems and thought pattern's and replace them with what is either revealed to you or what is written as you read and study the Bible.

When it comes to your mind in the matter, this

is where all of your battles, fights, and struggles will begin. If I could say one thing about having a relationship with God, it would be: The purpose of our relationship [salvation] is to change the way we think, react to, and perceive the world we live in (which will one-day pass away), and to prepare your heart, mind, and soul for a life of eternity with God.

In the beginning of this chapter, I said that Satan tries to control your mind because he wants access to your heart. He wants to desensitize your spirit and heighten your emotions. If Satan can influence your flesh, he will deter you from the righteousness of God working in and on you. Satan gains access to your heart by implanting a thought. Then that thought produces an emotion, and that emotion produces an action. When he produces or tries to plant a thought, ten times out of ten, he is appealing to your flesh. You must guard your mind, specifically your thoughts.

Casting down imaginations, and every high thing that exalteth itself against the knowledge of God and bringing into captivity every thought to the obedience of Christ.

2 Corinthians 10:5 K.J.V.

The first time I read that scripture I was like, "Do what with what?" Bringing every thought into captivity and making it obedient to Christ (Wipe's forehead and takes a deep breath), sounds hard? It was for me at first as well. I'm going to give you a technique that was introduced to me. It's been very helpful to me and I still use it to this day. It's a challenge at first, but once you continue to practice it, it becomes less of a challenge, and more of a habit.

When Satan introduces a thought to you, you simply replace it with a different thought. Not any thought will do, you need a thought with power—The Word of God [Scripture]. After Jesus' baptism by John, he was led into the wilderness to be tempted by Satan. When Satan introduced the temptations to Him, Christ replied with the Word of God, stating It Is Written, rather "God said!". Remember the legality of the Word. If you can take that "sin rooted" thought and replace it with a "Word (Biblical) rooted" thought, you will then produce a "Biblical rooted" response/emotion, and then an action that is in alignment and agreement with God. When you replace a sinful thought with a Biblical thought, the character and mind of Christ begins to become evident in your life, your spirit grows stronger, and your soul begins its conversion.

Your old nature went from thought to emotion, and from emotion to action. In Christ, you go from thought to the Word of God, from the Word of God to the fruit of the Spirit, and in the fruit of the Spirit you respond. Whatever transformation comes from you bringing the sinful thought into subjection, should produce one of these characteristics in which you respond in.

But the Holy Spirit produces this kind of fruit in our lives: love, joy, peace, patience, kindness, goodness, faithfulness, 23 gentleness, and self-control.

Galatians 5:22 N.L.T.

Your response should be in love, respond in joy, respond in peace, respond in self- control, etc. You are no longer responding in your emotions that will deter you off of the path of God, but you are responding in a way that pleases Him, by being in agreement with His Spirit.

Study to shew thyself approved unto God, a workman that needeth not to be ashamed, rightly dividing [holding a straight course] [to] the word of truth 2 Timothy 2:15 K.J.V.

If you do not feed your spirit with the Word, when the enemy comes and implants that thought— what will you fight with if your reserves are empty? You will be left defenseless against him, and more than likely you will sin. When you meditate and gain understanding from the Word, and pray, Satan cannot gain access to your heart through your mind, because the thought does not produce an emotion. Therefore, it cannot produce an action. Stay alert because he will try and find a thought that gets your attention, and that is his way into your heart and life.

You must bring every thought that comes across your mind under the influence of the Word of God! Do not let any thought linger. My pastor often quotes his father in saying, "You can't control where a bird lands, but you can control where it builds its nest!" 10 out of 10, you cannot control the thoughts that enter your mind. It is a part of human nature. However, you can control how long that thought stays there, and how big it grows. The vulnerability of a thought life unguarded is detrimental to the entryway of your heart. We have all been there, thought about something too long that it changed the way we felt and behaved. Your thought life controls your demeanor. As a believer, we are called to carry the demeanor of Christ Jesus, which is of Grace and Truth. The only way that this is possible is to bring your thoughts under subjection to the Word of God. As your thought life transforms, so will you.

Going forth, begin to train your mind and your thoughts to only reiterate what that Word of God says about you, your life, and the situations you face. You will know the thoughts that are not of God, which are being revealed to you by the reading of the Word and prayer. You can even begin to do this for your loved ones. Speak it, and then pray it daily and throughout the day. This is not a one-time event, but a habitual practice that will turn into a lifestyle and a more fulfilling life for you. Every Christian needs it from the pulpit to the door. Satan knows the validity and the power behind the way your thoughts can alter your life, actions, and decisions. Remember, his job is to kill, steal, and destroy! If he can get your actions to reflect your thought life, then he has won. Do not let him win!

Lastly, the author of the letter to the Philippian church encourages you to do this:

Finally, brethren,

Whatsoever things are true,

Whatsoever things are honest,

Whatsoever things are just,

Whatsoever things are pure,

Whatsoever things are lovely,

Whatsoever things are of a good report; If there be any virtue, and if there be any praise,

THINK ON THESE THINGS!

Philippians 4:8 K.J.V.

Type A Warrior: Contemplates or Makes Decisions Based on Emotions

TACTIC #1: SABOTAGE

> Sabotage:
> Any underhand interference with production as by enemy agents during wartime.

Satan wants to sabotage your relationship with God by influencing the desires of your flesh and emotions through your thought life. If he can antagonize your thoughts, he can influence your emotions thereby creating an action that leads to sin and spiritual death, pulling away from Holy Spirit.

His goal is to ultimately sever your intimacy with God and lead you away from Him as he did with Adam and Eve.

Defense:

- Read and study the Word of God!
- Pray the Word of God!
- Be mindful of the thoughts that are lingering in your mind. If they are not Biblically based, replace them with a relevant scripture.
- Keep your heart and motives pure!
- Yield and Obey to the leading of Holy Spirit in what He is revealing to you about you!

    1 John 5:3

    2 John 1:4

    2 Thessalonians 3:3-5

    Psalm 24

    Psalm 51

Prayer:

Heavenly Father, forgive me of my sins and I forgive those who sinned against me. I know that You have called me to live righteously before You, and to love You with all my heart, and I'm sorry if I haven't been showing You through my actions. Today I rededicate my life and my love to you. Change my desires to be transformed into yours. Create in me a pure heart and help me discipline my thoughts towards an outward expression of my love for You in my actions. Give me the desire to learn and follow all of Your requirements, decrees, laws, and commands. Put them into my mind and write them on my heart. I thank You that I have the mind of Christ that allows me to guard and change my thoughts to Your "Word rooted" thoughts, producing the fruit of the Spirit, then "Word rooted" actions. Let the fruits of my actions be in alignment with the fruit of Your Word.

In Jesus' name I pray, Amen.

Section Five:

Don't Abort

TYPE B WARRIOR

"**L**earn from other people's mistakes" was a popular saying when I was growing up, but how true is it? It was often coupled with the story of the hot stove: If Susie touched the hot stove and got burned, knowing Susie got burned, should incline you not to touch the hot stove. How many of us touched the hot stove anyway? (Raising my hand!)

> Type B Warrior: Makes Decisions Based on the Faith of Others

When I asked Ian, what was going through his mind throughout this whole ordeal, he told me, "Nothing". He said he had so much faith in my faith that he didn't even stop to consider there was anything wrong.

Do not put your trust in princes, in human beings, who cannot save.

Psalm 146:3 N.I.V

In your own personal battle of redefining your relationship with God, you must be able to sustain your own faith. Depending on someone else's faith and experiences, will only set you up for failure. Yes, to hear the testimonies of others should encourage you, but they are to help increase YOUR faith in YOUR personal walk with Christ. No two people are exactly alike. No two people perceive things the exact same way. No two people have the exact same experiences. If this is true, how can you fight Spiritual Warfare relying on someone else's faith?

TACTIC #2 ABORT

I found myself on a nature trail one day. I just wanted to get out of the house and go somewhere that I could spend time with the Holy Spirit, and really talk to Him. I needed a place free from the influence of my home environment. Halfway through the walk I made this confession, "I just want to get to a place in God where I don't need faith to survive anymore!" My mindset was this—I was tired of going through different tests and trials, tired of not having enough, and depending on God for everything, and I mean everything. I was a single mom, no job, taking care of my children, one child with special needs, and on a limited income. Everything we have and accomplished was because we trusted that God would take care of us, and He did. We didn't always get everything we wanted, but we always had everything we needed.

Now you may think, well, what's wrong with that? God always provided, didn't He? And I will say, "Yes, He did, but it came at a cost. A lot of prayer, a lot of fasting, and a lot of dying to self". I was tired, exhausted, and wanted this to end.

The Holy Ghost response to my confession was simply this, "Without faith it's impossible to please God! When the Son of man returns shall He find faith in the earth realm. From beginning to the end faith is necessary!". I thought to myself, "Man I'll never win this battle," but my mouth said, "Boy, God is a hard man!". Just when I said this, the Holy Spirit reminded me of those very same words of the servant who had buried his one talent.

Then the servant with one talent came and said, "Master, I knew you were a harsh man, harvesting crops you didn't plant, and gathering crops you didn't cultivate.

Matthew 25:24 K.J.V.

Immediately I began to repent. I had become that perverse and wicked servant. I was unsatisfied with my one talent, unsatisfied with what the Lord had entrusted to me—Faith.

The parable of the talents can be found in *Matthew 25* and *Luke 19*. As you familiarize yourself with this story, you'll read that the Master had given to his three servants talents, money. To one he gave five, to another he gave two, and the other he gave one talent. According to Holman's Illustrated Bible Dictionary, a talent was a unit of measurement in Biblical times usually weighing 58-80 pounds. One talent of silver was worth more than 15 years' wages. One talent of gold was worth even more (You Version Bible App, 1996, Matthew 25 verse15).

Paul writes: *For I say, through the grace given unto me, to every man that is among you, not to think of himself more highly than he ought to think; but to think soberly, according as God hath dealt to every man the measure of faith.*

Romans 12:3 K.J.V.

"Rumika, I want you to see that one talent as faith," the Holy Spirit says to me. Faith is the currency by which we communicate our needs and desires to God, having total trust in His understanding, and belief in His eternal purpose, plan, and will. Revisiting the parable of the talents: two out of the three servants were commended for their works, while the last one was condemned. Many have preached and taught on this scriptural text, and all that I've heard condemned also this servant that buried his one talent. We are ever so encouraged not to be like this one servant. I believe that we have misunderstood this poor man, and what he was faced with. Having walked about 60 seconds in his sandals, I offered up this rebuttal on his behalf—he was frustrated.

In verse *15 of Matthew 25*, it tells you the master gave each servant his proportion based on their abilities. As a believer, and a new believer, it is so easy for you to get caught up in the "high life" of Christendom. Walking and operating in the power of God, functioning in the spiritual gifts, and/or the prosperity of God's blessings without giving second thought to the cost of the process. Your main objective as a believer is to secure your eternal spot in heaven by having a daily relationship with God the Father through Christ. As you spend more time with the Lord via the Holy Ghost, you mature in Christ, and the Holy Ghost activates and leads you to more mature matters of the Kingdom. Sometimes it may become overwhelming and frustrating when you cannot see the result or the fruits of your spiritual walk, and you find yourself burying your faith Some time ago, before my nature trail conversation with the Holy Spirit, He'd used the same parable to teach me confidence. As I was reading the scripture earlier that year, He asked me, "How did the servants know what to do with the money when the master left?" I went back to the text and reread it. I reread it again and again, over and over, searching for some hidden clue. After about the fourth attempt, I gave in and asked, "How?". His response was, "The servants spent much time with their master. They observed him, his ways, and his habits. They had spent much time studying and paying attention to their master that when he left, they knew exactly what to do in his absence." When he returned, all but one had something to show for it. You see, the master in this parable is Jesus, and the servants are us! According to Romans 12:3, God has given unto each one of us a measure of faith, and this parable tells us, he does according to our abilities. God will not call you to a place that you do not have the faith to be sustained in. What He will do is process you to that place and allow your faith and understanding to grow with you. You charge your faith, by gaining knowledge and understanding through the amount of time you spend with the Holy Spirit in the Word.

HOLY SPIRIT

Now I want to make a pit stop here and explain the role of the Holy Ghost/ Holy Spirit (used interchangeably) in your life. Now within these last paragraphs, I have recapped conversations between the Holy Ghost and I. Strange? It should not be. For this very reason is He here, to make known to you the mysteries of heaven, bring understanding to the Word of God and God, and aid you in everyday life. Jesus tells us this about the Holy Ghost:

If ye love me, keep my commandments. And I will pray for the Father, and He shall give you another Comforter, that he may abide with you forever.

John 14:15-16 K.J.V.

But the Comforter, which is the Holy Ghost, whom the Father will send in my name, He shall teach you all things, and bring all things to your remembrance, whatsoever I have said unto you.

John 14:26 K.J.V.

According to the Book of John, one of the first names given to the Holy Spirit is Comforter. First and foremost, I want you to understand, the Holy Spirit is a comforter sent to comfort you with the peace of Christ throughout life. Second, He is your teacher. Simply put, the disciples had Jesus, we have the Holy Ghost! He is your teacher, your comforter, your counselor, and your friend. Every believer in the faith of Christ, has free access to the Holy Spirit. He is given as a gift upon the confession and receipt of salvation.

I just Don't Get it?

And you also were included in Christ when you heard the message of truth, the gospel of your salvation. When you believed, you were marked in Him with a seal, the promised Holy Spirit, who is a deposit guaranteeing our inheritance until the redemption of those who are God's possession to the praise of His glory.

Ephesians 1:13-14 N.I.V.

The Holy Spirit is a He, not an it! He is one of the three parts of the Holy Trinity—The Father, the Son, and the Holy Spirit. He is a person. He has a job, and a role just as the Father and the Son does. The Father's role is to show you the loving and caring character of God, the Son's role is to show you the selfless and sacrificial love of God, and the role of the Holy Spirit is to bring you into the revelation of God, the Father, and the Son Jesus Christ. He is here to impart unto you an understanding of Truth that will sustain you in this life and prepare you for the next.

You probably have had interactions with the Holy Spirit and did not yet realize it! Ever had an inner voice tell you to do something, or not go somewhere? Later when you see the effects of your obedience or disobedience you said to yourself, "Something told me to do that!" or "Something told me not to go there!". That something is not something, but a someone, the Holy Ghost! He speaks to your conscience, and the more you mature in the things of the Spirit, He becomes your conscience. Check out how Paul describes this to the Romans:

When outsiders [those not familiar with the voice of the Holy Spirit] who have never heard of God's law follow it more or less by instinct, they confirm its truth by their obedience. They show that God's law is not something alien, imposed on us from without, but woven into the very fabric of our creation [conscience]. There is something deep within them that echoes God's yes and no, right and wrong.

106

Romans 2:14-15 MSG.

You may have been using your conscience as your moral compass. Yet, the Bible tells you that your conscience was inscribed with God's yes and no and His right and wrong. What you perceive as your natural conscience is your God given conscience and you become more aware of it when you accept Christ as your Lord and Savior and equips you to follow the leading of the Holy Ghost. You can become more aware of the Holy Ghost by first praying and asking Him to make Himself known to you. Now I must warn, He is the Holy Spirit, but He is still God. He cannot be summoned or conjured up. Let your request be known and be patient. Wait on Him to reveal Himself to you.

Nevertheless, I tell you the truth; It is expedient for you that I go away: for if I go not away, the Comforter will not come unto you; but if I depart, I will send Him unto you. Howbeit when He, the Spirit of truth, is come, He will guide you into all truth: for He shall not speak of Himself; but whatsoever He shall hear, that shall He speak: and He will shew you things to come.

John 16:7, 13 K.J.V.

When Jesus was preparing His disciples for His death, resurrection, and eventually His return to heaven, they were really sad, but He was excited! He said to them, "I must go, that He may come." Jesus knew that the miracles He performed and the life of righteous, holiness, and obedience He lived was all because of the Holy Ghost. His disciples had not fully grasped this concept, yet Jesus was preparing them for His coming. Jesus had been the means in which His disciples and the people experienced God. He knew that it was in God's plan to restore man back to a one-on-one relationship with Him, no middleman, and in order for that to happen, Jesus had to return to heaven, and the Holy Spirit had to come down.

I just Don't Get it?

No longer will they teach their neighbor, or say to one another, "Know the Lord," because they will all know me, from the least of them to the greatest.

Hebrews 8:11 N.I.V.

The Holy Spirit makes your relationship with God tangible and real. Right now, in this dispensation of time, He is the link between God and man. We honor God. We pray to the Father. Abide by the teachings of Christ and live through the Holy Ghost. The Holy Spirit speaks to you always through the Word of God. ALL of God's Word [the Bible] is truth. To become familiar with the voice and the leading of the Holy Ghost, you must become familiar with scripture. It is through the Word of God that the Holy Spirit makes himself known. He can only teach you through the scripture you have exposed to your mind and heart. He can only bring to remembrance what you have studied and read. He can only reveal the depth of truth to you through Biblical scripture.

Jesus says,

"I AM the Way, I AM the Truth, and I AM the life. No one comes to the Father except through me." John 14:6.

The Holy Spirit reveals truth, in and through the Word.

But when the Comforter is come, whom I will send unto you from the Father, even the Spirit of truth, which proceedeth from the Father, He shall testify of me [Jesus].

John 15:26 K.J.V.

So, what does all this have to do with faith???

Faith comes by hearing and hearing by the Word of God.

Romans 10:17 K.J.V.

Or you can requote the scripture as, Faith comes by hearing, and hearing the voice of Holy Ghost. It is the voice of the Holy Ghost, and your familiarization with the Word of God, that solidifies and strengthens your faith. As you spend time with the Holy Ghost, truth is revealed, and you become enlightened about the reality of God! Remember, Faith is the currency by which we communicate our needs and desires to God, having total trust in His understanding, belief in His eternal purpose, plan, and will. Without this component [the Holy Spirit and the Words] of faith your relationship and communication [prayers] is nullified. They mean nothing. The second tactic Satan uses against us believers is deception. If he can distort your faith, he will minimize your communication with God. If he can minimize your communication, he can lead you away from God. Satan is your enemy. He comes to steal, kill and destroy. His objective is and will always be to pull you away from God. He wants you to abort your faith, abort your relationship, abort your salvation. He does this by using spirits (influences) of doubt and deception that pry at your confidence.

> Your faith is tied to your belief, and what you believe is tied to your trust.

Faith essentially believes that God will do what He said He will do (written or spoken) when there is yet no tangible manifestation of what He has said. Your belief in who God is, strengthens your faith in what He can do. This is why the Holy Spirit is important to your walk and your faith. He strengthens your belief in who God is. You feed your faith by reading and studying the Bible, which expresses and teaches you the character of God, as well as teaching you the promises of God. God desires you to believe in Him, as well as believe and trust Him.

Part of Satan's deception is getting you to believe that you cannot have a relationship with God, it is hard to trust God, or God does not want to have a relationship with you. It's all a lie! I found out some time ago this truth. Relationships are built on intimacy, and intimacy is strengthened when secrets of the heart and mind are revealed. Have you ever been in love, or had a crush? What about a friendship that you have cherished and honored over the years? Think about all the moments that captured your heart in those relationships, and made you say or think, "This is why I love you!". I can almost guarantee that those times are centered around that individual sharing with you a piece of their heart or a piece of their mind that they do not share with just anyone, but they've chosen to share it with you, and vice versa.

The secret things belong to God, but those things which He revealed belong to us and to our children forever, that we may do all the words of this law.

Deuteronomy 29:29 N.K.J.V

Can you solve the mysteries of God? Can you discover everything about the Almighty?

Job 11:7 N.L.T.

...that their hearts may be encouraged, being knit together in love, and attaining to all riches of the full assurance of understanding, to the knowledge of the mystery of God, both of the Father and Christ.

Colossians 2:2 N.K.J.V.

As you read and study your Bible, you will begin to receive understanding of what is written. You will find yourself having an Aha moment saying, "OMGosh I never understood that before!", or "Oh, that's what that means!". In those moments, the Holy Spirit is enlightening your hearts with God's truth! In those

110

moments God is sharing His heart and mind with you. (I always get teary eyed thinking about this). God is so big, so vast, at times it feels like why would He care about little ole me. You are so important to God. You are so loved and cherished by Him. Satan never wants you to come to and hold onto this truth, and to solidify His love and trust with you, God allows Holy Spirit to reveal to you the hidden mysteries in His Word stemming from His heart and mind. God trusts you enough to reveal His heart and mind to you. He trusts that you will abide by and obey what He has shown you, and in return He wants you to trust Him.

Trust in the Lord with all your heart and lean not on your own understanding; in all your ways acknowledge Him, and He shall direct your paths.

Proverbs 3:5 N.K.J.V.

God is so concerned about you, and so in love with you. He wants to know everything on your heart and mind. You may say He is God, and He knows everything. True enough, but He wants to hear it from you. He wants to hear about your day, what is worrying, why you are sad. He wants to hear about that hard decision you must make. When you are happy, He wants to hear about that too! By telling God what's on your heart and mind you are simultaneously acknowledging His existence and presence and inviting Him into comfort, love, and direct you. So, don't hold back anymore! Grow in the reciprocity of a Trust relationship between you and God! When you want to strengthen your faith, turn to the Word of God, but when God wants to strengthen your faith, He presents you with obstacles and trials.

In my former youth group, as an ice breaker, we played this game. One person would get blindfolded, and their teammate had to lead them around the youth room in an allotted amount of time.

The lights were off, kids were screaming, and music was playing. The duo that completed the race in the shortest amount of time won! It was hilarious watching the blindfolded person attempt to make his/her way around the room by listening to the directions of their team member. Every now and again someone would shout out the wrong direction. The blindfolded individual had to listen intently as they attempted to decipher through the noise and follow the correct directions of their partner. It was a lot of fun and entertaining but proven to be very difficult. I was so caught up in the excitement of the game then, that I didn't pay attention to the spiritual application it had. Our leaders were imparting to us how to overcome adversities by recognizing and listening intently for God's voice, instructions and directions; trusting, believing, and having faith in Him even though we could not see our surroundings or what lay ahead of us. The team that always won was usually a duo who were good friends, they knew each other, they had intimacy and understanding.

But we rejoice in our sufferings, because we know that suffering produces endurance; endurance [produces] character; and character [produces] hope.

Romans 5:3-4 N.I.V.

There are two types of trials I want you to become familiar with: Internal trials and External trials. Your external trials are what God uses to build your faith, and your internal trials are what builds your character. Character is very important in terms of what sets you apart as an individual and a Christ Follower. It moves beyond you being labeled a good person. Your character incorporates all your distinguishing qualities and traits. From the time you were born until now your character has been groomed through the influence of your family, friends, society, and education. These influences, through the decisions you have made, according to your desires (mind, will, and emotions) are what makes you, you. The good and the bad. Your character is the mindset you operate from. God's goal for you on earth is for you to become the embodiment of Christ. His desire for you is to take on the character of Christ. The mind of Christ.

Let this mind be in you, which was also in Christ Jesus.

Philippians 2:5 K.J.V.

He doesn't want to change the essence of who you are because you were created in His image and in His likeness, but He wants you to see and become who you really are through Christ Jesus. There are qualities and traits locked inside of you put there by your Creator before you were born, Psalm 139, and He would like to unlock those traits, qualities, and giftings if you would allow Him.

INTERNAL TRIALS

Your internal trials are two-fold. They target your self-esteem and self-image issues that deal with your identity, and they deal with the temptations that you face in transitioning from your old lifestyle. Clarity and understanding in both of these fundamentals build and strengthen your character, how you perceive and feel about yourself. You may have a poor image of yourself or you may even lack self-love. How do you get to the place where you are comfortable and confident in the skin that you are in? You have to go on a journey of self-discovery, you have to find out who you are. As a Christ-follower what you identify with, and who you identify as is very vital. Ask yourself these questions: Who or what is defining you? Who or what is shaping your identity?

SELF-IMAGE, IDENTITY, AND PURPOSE

As a Christian you take credence to the truth that you are God's creation, created in His image and likeness.

So, God created man in His own image; in the image of God He created him; male and female He created them.

Genesis 1: 27 N.K.J.V.

You are a child of God by grace through faith and a joint heir with Jesus Christ. You are an alien to this world, a pilgrim passing through. The Bible tells us that wherever your treasure is, your heart will be there also *Matthew 6:21*. We have this saying, "Home is where the heart is!". Your home, your treasure is with God Elohim, and you identify with the Kingdom of Heaven. When you gave your life to Jesus by accepting Him into your heart as your

Lord and Savior, you transitioned from a one-dimensional living to a two-dimensional living.

They are not of the world, just as I [Jesus] am not of the world. Sanctify them [Father] by Your truth. Your word is truth.

John 17:16 N.K.J.V.

And do not be conformed to this world, but be transformed by the renewing of your mind, that you may prove what is that good and acceptable and perfect will of God.

Romans 12:2 N.K.J.V.

Dear friends, I warn you as "temporary residents and foreigners" to keep away from worldly desires that wage war against your very souls.

1 Peter 2:11 N.L.T.

Friends, this world is not your home, so don't make yourselves cozy in it.

1 Peter 2:11 MSG

I go to prepare a place for you. And if I go and prepare a place for you, I will come again and receive you to Myself; that where I am, there you may be also.

John 14:2c and 3 N.K.J.V.

This two-dimensional living is what makes us aware of the spiritual forces at hand and gives us a hope that there is a place that God has prepared for those who are His and have lived a life of love and devotion to Him. Therefore, you do not identify with this world, you identify with Christ, who is the first born of many brethren baptized in the Holy Ghost and received a glory not of this world but of God. You are a son of God.

For as many as are led by the Spirit of God, these are sons of God.

Romans 8:14 N.K.J.V.

And I am certain that God, who began the good work within you, will continue his work until it is finally finished on the day when Christ Jesus returns.

Philippians 1:6 N.L.T.

Your identity is continuously being revealed to you as you empty yourself of the desires of this world and grow in the principles, understanding, and desires of God's Kingdom. You are referred to as a son in the Bible because you are aiming to live a life that pleases God the Father. You honor Him by loving Him with everything in you, obeying the teachings of Christ, seeking after Him with a pure heart, and loving others as just as you love yourself. Because you spend so much time seeking after Him, pursuing Him to know more about Him, He in turns reveals to you your purpose which is connected to your identity. You cannot effectively and fully operate in your purpose if you do not know who you are. For example, I am a child of God and I am fulfilling my purpose as an author in writing this series to help other spiritually young believers obtain a greater understanding in the faith that God has called us to. Your journey in finding out your purpose begins with understanding where you came from, your roots, and history.

Therefore, if anyone is in Christ, he is a new creation; old things have passed away; behold, all things have become new.

2 Corinthians 5:17 N.K.J.V.

And do not be conformed to this world, but be transformed by the renewing of your mind, that you may prove what is that good and acceptable and perfect will of God.

Romans 12:2 N.K.J.V

In order to be a good son, you must understand and learn your history. Not the ancestral history of your mother and father, but the history of the relationship between God and mankind. From the Book of Genesis to Revelation the Bible gives an account of this history through stories and the lives of others. Take time out to get to know your history. 2 *Corinthians* says that because you are now in Christ, you are a new person. All of the old factors which shaped who you were before coming into the knowledge of Christ has passed away, and now it's time for you to learn where you came from, and who God really created you to be! Some things will be taught, and a lot more is revealed. The Holy Spirit teaches and reveals as you read and study the Word. Even when you attend Bible Study at your home church, the Holy Spirit uses your Pastor to teach you the scripture. Other components are revealed in your personal study time.

There are great many mysteries in the Word of God. These mysteries are revealed on the basis of an intimate relationship with God. It is the revelation of the Word of God, that solidifies your faith and your identity in Christ. In the secret place is where God reveals the secret things. We all struggle with defining who we are at one time or another. I believe it is due in part to the lie that we think we have to serve only one purpose. My purpose is to empower women of all ages and the people of God and I do that through writing, poetry, and mentorships. These are the purposes that I serve God in the capacity of the giftings He has bestowed on me, and that's not even the whole list! Your poor self-image and self-esteem are due to the fact that you have not fully grasped your identity in Christ, it has nothing to do with your outward appearance. I promise you this one thing: go deeper in your knowledge about your God history and in the understanding of who God says you are and your God confidence will reveal your true purpose and make you feel a whole lot better about yourself!

Therefore, do not cast away your confidence, which has great reward.

Hebrews 10:35 N.K.J.V.

TEMPTATION AND FASTING

Secondly, in dealing with internal trials that build your character, come in the form of temptations. Whenever you succumb to your temptations, it is very important you take responsibility for your actions. Ask for forgiveness and repent. To repent means to turn away or go the opposite direction of. Temptations are not to be taken lightly. The detriment to their effects is strong. They are powerful urges that come back from your old lifestyle and desires that haunts you like symptoms of withdrawal that need a fix. Every believer has temptations and has fallen to them. All of us! The key is not to make a lifestyle out of them (sin), but to know how to fight them. I have cried many times on occasions when I have fallen to the temptations of my past. Before I rededicated my life back to Christ, I was a sexually active person who did drugs, as I mentioned in the first half of this book. Quite naturally my strongest temptations came in the form of sexual urges and the need to smoke. While I did not resolve to having sex, and smoking weed again, I masturbated and smoked cigarettes. Every time like clockwork the temptations would come, and I would resist them as I was taught, but it would only work for a couple of hours, sometimes a day or so, but I would always find

118

myself in the need of a fix, so I would give in. I would feel so disgusted, racked with shame, and I condemned myself.

In order to win battles against the cravings of your old/carnal nature, you must fast. Fasting is abstaining from food and/or water for a designated period of time. Fasting is a practice that all believers should incorporate in their lifestyle. When you fast, a supernatural transition takes place. Remember spiritual warfare are the battles we cannot hear, touch, or see. When we walk according to the truth of God's Word, these battles are always won in our favor, through faith by grace.

Remember, when you are being tempted, do not say, "God is tempting me." God is never tempted to do wrong, and He never tempts anyone else. Temptations comes from our own desires, which entice us and drags us away.

James 1:13-14 N.L.T.

Overcoming temptations by fasting is a form of engaging in spiritual warfare. Temptations are more than mere thoughts that come up and are planted into your mind. You cannot replace these types of thoughts with the Word of God, to produce a different emotion that changes the course of your actions. Temptations are strong, powerful urges that affect your mind, emotions, and body simultaneously. They are the desires of your old self trying to creep back into your life of righteousness in Christ. In dealing with temptations, understand that your desire to live godly, holy, and righteously are under attack and on trial daily. You win these battles through fasting. Fasting is a spiritual tool based on the principle of reciprocity. When done properly, you are shifting the domineering power from your carnal nature to your spirit man.

Walk in the Spirit, and ye shall not fulfill the lust [desires] of the flesh.

Galatians 5:16 K.J.V.

Biblical fasting is not just abstaining from food. When you weaken one nature you must strengthen the other. You refuse yourself eating, which weakens your physical body, and you feed your spirit man through prayer and reading the Word. Your physical body requires physical food, but your spiritual self requires spiritual food. This strengthens your spirit man, the part of you that is connected to God. What takes place during your time of fasting is a bonding of your spirit with the Holy Spirit, and He empowers you from within, so that every action and decision you make is influenced by the Truth [Christ], and the Word of God. As the direction of your decisions begin to shift, your Christ-like character is being groomed and strengthened. This gratifies the Holy Ghost, glorifies God, and edifies you as a believer.

When you follow the desires of your sinful nature, the results are very clear: sexual immorality, impurity, lustful pleasures, idolatry, sorcery, hostility, quarreling, jealousy, outbursts of anger, selfish ambition, dissension, division, envy, drunkenness, wild parties, and other sins like these.

Galatians 5:19-21 N.L.T.

But the Holy Spirit produces this kind of fruit in our lives: love, joy, peace, patience, kindness, goodness, faithfulness, gentleness, and self-control. There is no law against these things! Those who belong to Christ Jesus have nailed the passions and desires of their sinful nature to his cross and crucified them there. Since we are living by the Spirit, let us follow the Spirit's leading in every part of our lives.

Galatians 5:22-25 N.L.T.

You will face temptations daily! But this does not mean that you must fast every day of the year. Fasting is a lifestyle, not an event. It's not something that you do when you're in trouble, but a habit that you put into practice! You should set aside time monthly or weekly to fast along with reading the Word, and prayer. Fasting without the Word and prayer is simply dieting. To reap the full benefits of Biblical fasting you must incorporate Bible reading/studying and prayer. Find scriptures relating to your situation and meditate on them. Understand what the scriptures are saying and pray them over your life! The decisions that you make in the face of temptation reveals the value that you have put on your relationship with God. Is your fix worth more to you than your closeness to God? Is it worth more to you than maturing in things of Christ? This is the question you should ask yourself. Be honest with God, be honest with yourself. You will struggle, but fight! A struggle is not just a battling of thoughts in your mind, but an inward outcry for change. Fasting has many benefits outside of aiding you in overcoming your temptations. When you fast correctly you build up a spiritual sensitivity and discernment [discussed in the next section], which allows you to hear and communicate with the Holy Spirit with clarity and understanding. Having an unobstructed line of communication with the Holy Ghost has benefits that cannot be numbered!

EXTERNAL TRIALS

The second type of trials are external trials, and these may come in diverse forms, from personal sickness/ illness of a loved one to financial disparity. They present themselves in situations and circumstances that are difficult to deal with mentally and emotionally. We know that a Type B Warrior reacts based on someone else's faith/experiences. Now you're facing your trial and you have to make a decision or choice, how does someone else's faith and ability benefit you at this time mentally, physically, spiritually, or even emotionally? It doesn't! Sure, their testimony may encourage you and give you insight on how to deal, but you cannot use their faith. Witnessing their faith at work may encourage you in your faith.

If you do not stand firm in faith, you will not stand at all.

Isaiah 7:9c N.I.V.

If ye will not believe, surely ye shall not be established.

Isaiah 7:9c K.J.V.

Also, that

Consequently, faith comes from hearing the message, and the message is heard through the word about Christ.

Romans 10:17N.I.V.

Let us revisit the game again, now faith is the blindfold. You are the blindfolded person and you have chosen a partner. You're putting on that blindfold [Faith]. You believe your partner will lead you correctly, you trust them, and you hold them to their word.

Now, let us stop and think for a second. Would you put on that blindfold if you doubted this person for any tiny reason? If you had an inch of doubt about their capabilities, you would be standing there trying to decipher within yourself if it would be wise for you to ultimately trust this person. Now imagine God as your partner, and you have an honest doubt about your security in the relationship. Your doubt has just turned to unbelief, and your unbelief, believe it or not is a sin.

But let him ask in faith, nothing wavering. For he that wavereth is like a wave of the sea driven with the wind and tossed... A double minded man is unstable in all his ways.

James 1:6, 8 K.J.V.

For whatever is not from faith is sin.

Romans 14:23b N.K.J.V.

If you do not believe God, you will not follow Him or His instructions. Doubt is a mechanism that Satan uses to manipulate you to render you dysfunctional and impotent. Did you know, in correlation to the Word of God, Faith is your next mightiest weapon against Satan?

In addition to all this [the armor of God] take up the shield of faith, with which you can extinguish all the flaming arrows of the evil one.

Ephesians 6:16 N.I.V.

Once you have the Word embedded in you, you will also need to believe [have faith and trust] in the Word in which you have read and studied, and that which was taught to you and revealed by the Holy Ghost. In the midst of the challenges that life will throw at you, your hope must be anchored in something.

I just Don't Get it?

Now faith is the substance of things hoped for, the evidence of things not seen.

Hebrews 11:1 N.K.J.V.

Over the years I had struggled with this scripture, faith in correlation with hope. I could never grasp its meaning in how it was supposed to help me understand faith. Until recently, the Holy Spirit gave me the revelation of this scripture's meaning. The concept did not lie in grasping the concept of faith, but the concept of hope. Hope is that very thing, the idea that you hold onto that gives you strength to keep going. It is the very place from where your faith is born. The scripture says that faith is the substance of things hoped for. I want to focus on three words in that phrase: Faith, Substance, and Hope. Hope is that internal belief to see a thing manifest. The Substance is what you want to see manifest, and faith is the combination of both. Therefore, your faith is your internal belief to see a "thing" manifest. Here's the tricky part.

Therefore, do not be foolish and thoughtless, but understand and firmly grasp what the will of the Lord is.

Ephesians 5:17 AMP

In order for your faith to give birth to the manifested substance you hoped for, it must be in alignment with God's will. And you find God's will hidden in the mysteries of scripture revealed to you by Holy Ghost. What you hope for must be revealed as God's desire for you.

But without faith it is impossible to please God,

for he that cometh to God must believe that he is, and that he is a rewarder of them that diligently seek him. Hebrews 11:6 K.J.V.

First and foremost, your faith should be rooted and grounded in your salvation, meaning that the most important substance that you can hold onto is the belief [hope] that God will make good on His promise that you will die in Christ also being resurrected in Christ into eternal life, your reward. Eternal life is real. We will all die and wake up in either heaven or hell and remain there for eternity. Secondly, you will need your faith every day. Everyday there ought to be something that you are believing for God to do for you!

Beloved, I pray that in every way you may succeed and prosper and be in good health [physically], just as [I know] your soul prospers [spiritually].

3 John 1:2 AMP

God your Father is very much concerned about your dayto-day affairs and wants you to include Him in them. Once you have established faith through salvation, He does not want you to throw away your faith, but to continue to use it so the will of heaven concerning you may be established in your life. This is all connected to your true identity and purpose revealed.

Trust in the Lord with all your heart; do not depend on your own understanding. Seek his will in all you do, and he will show you which path to take.

Proverbs 3:5-6 N.L.T.

There are two ways in which Satan uses doubt to take you off the paths that God has constructed for you. First, he will try to get you to doubt God or His Word. This is where you draw from the well of intimacy that you and God have shared. Draw from His love, and the moments of bonding over revelations from the Word. Do not allow Satan to dissuade you of God's love and draw you away from the relationship you guys have built. Kick him to the curb! Hold on to what was revealed/spoken to you. You may be believing God for a healing, finances, a spouse, deliverance for yourself or another. This is your substance. Find out what the Word of God says about your substance and hold tightly onto it. That is your hope. Your belief in what you hope for is what brings about a manifestation.

Sometimes God will answer you quickly, other times you are really going to need to rely on the strength of Holy Spirit to get you through that trial. Satan loves to stick doubt into the minds of God's people, especially when you are going through a trial, and it feels as if God has forgotten about you. He has not. Satan's lies sound like this:

God isn't going to come through for you

You are not worthy enough

He will do it for anyone but you

That's too big for God to do

You are hopeless, just give up

You are too deep in

All of these are Satan's lies, and he wants to demean you and God's relationship by distorting your faith. If what you thought about God, how you perceive Him, was not important, relevant, and effective in Spiritual Warfare, then why does Satan work overtime to kill your faith?? Replace every lie that Satan whispers in your ear with a Word rooted thought! You must persevere.

> Perseverance: "steady persistence in adhering to a course of action, a belief, or a purpose, steadfastness"
> Persistence: "refusing to give up or let go."
> (A.H.D.)

Second, Satan will try to get you to doubt yourself. If Satan cannot shake your faith in God, he will try to shake your faith in you. Why would Satan want you to doubt yourself? Let us go back to the game. Your blindfolded, and the blindfold represents your faith. God is your partner. You have spent some time with Him, you love Him, you trust Him, so y'all got this right? He is navigating through the plan that He has already constructed for you, but you're unfamiliar with the territory, it doesn't feel right, and you are a little afraid and hesitant. The onlookers, let's call them your old desires, are calling back to that place of familiarity. You still hear God's voice, but it's faint. You stop to ponder. You don't necessarily doubt God, but you begin to doubt your ability in what God has asked you to do. It feels much easier to go back to your old self, taking the easy way out. Now you're stagnated, you are not moving backward, and you're definitely not going forward, because of doubt in who God says you are, and fear.

Therefore, do not cast away your confidence, which has great reward. For you have need of endurance, so that after you have done the will of God, you may receive the promise.

Hebrews 10:35-36 N.K.J.V.

Who you are will always be challenged by Satan—ALWAYS! It is very important that you remember and affirm yourself as a son of God daily. Restate your purpose to yourself and ask Holy Spirit for ways that you can prepare for, fulfill, and walk in your purpose every day. Fear is a natural component that we all as believers and non-believers face, but fear is not from God. He does not want us to be afraid of anything or anyone. Fear is a crippling spirit. It stops you from reaching your full potential and fulfilling your purpose.

I just Don't Get it?

For God has not given us a spirit of fear, but of power and of love and of a sound mind.

1 Timothy 1:7 N.K.J.V.

For all creation is waiting eagerly for that future day when God will reveal who his children really are.

Romans 8:19 N.L.T.

There is a whole world out there waiting on you to discover and fulfill your purpose. You do not have to be afraid of who is against you because you know who you are! There is power in the knowledge that you have obtained that you are born of God and know Him. His love overflows towards you daily as you seek to do life with Him and trust Him. Your mind is solidified in His Word and promises as you renew it daily in the Word and pray. Be of courage, and charge on!

Have I not commanded you? Be strong and of good courage; do not be afraid, nor be dismayed, for the Lord your God is with you wherever you go.

Joshua 1:9
N.K.J.V.

I can do all things through Christ which strengtheneth me.

Philippians 4:13
K.J.V.

We have come to share in Christ, if we indeed hold [persevere, persist] our original confidence firm to the end.

Hebrews 3:14
E.S.V.

Walking in faith is having total trust in God's understanding, belief in His eternal purpose, plan, and will for your life, and having confidence in who you are in Him. Without these two it is impossible to please Him! Satan is very cunning. If he cannot get you to doubt God, he'll try to get you to doubt yourself. If you doubt yourself, you won't trust God. If you do not trust God, you won't believe Him. If you don't believe Him, then you do not have faith in Him. The blindfold comes off, and you're out the game, you lost the battle. Satan's ultimate goal is always to turn you away from God.

See to it, brothers [sisters], that none of you has a sinful, unbelieving heart that turns away from the living God.

Hebrews 3:12 N.I.V

Okay, so you have faith in God and confidence in your identity and purpose; What's next? How do you apply your faith engaging in Spiritual Warfare? I'm glad you asked.

What good is it, dear brothers, and sisters, if you say you have faith but don't show it by your actions? Can that kind of faith save anyone? Suppose you see a brother or sister who has no food or clothing, and you say, "Good-bye and have a good day; stay warm and eat well"— but then you don't give that person any food or clothing. What good does that do? So, you see, faith by itself isn't enough. Unless it produces good deeds, it is dead and useless.

James 2:14-17 K.J.V.

Faith without works is dead, we have all heard this scripture time and time again, but what does it really mean? In the aforementioned scripture, the writer is giving a comparison of how faith is to work. If you see someone in need, and you tell them to go in peace, but you have not equipped them to go in peace, then your words of peace mean nothing to them or their situation because you didn't do [action] anything to change it. Faith is the same way; you must couple it with action. In the previous scenario of the game, you did not follow through the instruction that God gave you, so your faith wasn't put into action; it was dead, and you lost that battle.

> WORKS
>
> **Natural**: "Deeds that you do towards others"
> **Spiritual Warfare**: "Assignment/ instructions from God."

Doing works [natural] is awesome. In fact, we as Christ Followers are supposed to have kind works. Befriending someone new to the neighborhood, offering kind words and encouragement, volunteering at a local charity, or helping someone in need, we are encouraged to let our good works shine.

In the same way, let your good deeds shine out for all to see, so that everyone will praise your heavenly Father.

Matthew 5:16 N.L.T.

Therefore, as we have opportunity, let us do good to all people, especially to those who belong to the family of believers.

Galatians 6:10 N.I.V.

In Spiritual Warfare it is not works [natural] that save you but works [spiritual] that makes you fruitful.

Now someone may argue, "Some people have faith; others have good deeds." But I say, "How can you show me your faith if you don't have good deeds? I will show you my faith by my good deeds.

James 2:18 N.L.T.

See the first man had works [natural] no faith, and the second man had works [spiritual] with faith. In facing your trials and tests, which do you think will equip you better to be an overcomer? Your works [spiritual]; they help bring the manifestation of what you hope for to pass.

Was not Abraham our father justified by works when he offered up His son Isaac on the altar? You see that his faith and his actions were working together, and faith was made complete by what he did... You see that a person is considered righteous by what they do and not by faith alone.

James 2:21-22, 24 E.S.V.

Abraham, whom we call the father of our faith, received an assignment, instructions from God to sacrifice his only son. The son in which God promised through him he would have many descendants. As you can imagine this had to be hard for Abraham to fathom, a perfect opportunity to doubt God or himself, yet Abraham trusted God and held onto the hope of the promise of many descendants revealed and spoken to Him by God.

...Abraham believed God, and it was credited to him as righteousness, and he was called God's friend.

James 2:23 E.S.V.

How do you activate your faith by your works?

But don't just listen to God's word. You must do what it says. Otherwise, you are only fooling yourselves.

James 1:22 N.L.T.

> Obedience
>
> DO what God instructs you to do. This is your works.

Side note: Obedience is very important in your walk in Christ—Very Important. Everything depends on it. *Romans 8:14 says, "Those who are led by the Spirit of God are sons of God."* It's like the game of following the leader. Whatever the Holy Spirit tells you to do, do it! Your life depends on it, your salvation depends on it, you obtain the promises in which you hope for in God depend on it. This is how you prove to God that you really trust Him.

Faith adheres to your spirit. The more you rely on God, the more you will be able to trust Him. You cannot operate/conquer in faith by looking at your trials in the physical. You will not be able to understand or overcome them. When you are walking by faith, you're being led by your God conscience—the Holy Spirit. When you begin to walk and follow through with the assignment/instructions the Holy Spirit has given you, your faith accelerates into works; then you will be able to see the physical manifestation of your faith.

I want to interject this little-known misunderstanding: every bad trial that you face is not from God. At times, because of your disobedience you leave doors to your life open, and Satan walks through those doors and wreaks havoc. When you find yourself going through a trial, ask yourself is God trying to build your faith or did you leave an open door due to disobedience. When you are walking in disobedience to the Holy Spirit, He convicts you, makes you feel bad about what you have done. Do not override this conviction. If you constantly override the Holy Spirit's conviction you will come numb to His corrections, and it will be harder for you to hear His voice. If you cannot hear His voice, then you cannot be led. If you are not being led, then you are not a son.

Before God can trust you with greater works, He has to test and build your faith. Your external trials condition your heart and mind to flow with God. This is effective by staying rooted and grounded in the Word of God and making it the hope that you connect to what you are believing Him to do. God foreknew you, *Jeremiah 1:5*, and also predestined you, *Romans 8:29*, you can conclude that He knows your limits as well. Not only does He know your limits, but He knows what it will take to bring you to the true revelation of who you are.

Blessed is the one who perseveres [refuse to let go] under trial because, having stood the test that person will receive the crown of life that the Lord has promised to those who love Him.

James 1:12 N.I.V.

Let perseverance finish its work so that you may be matured and complete, not lacking anything.

James 1:4 N.I.V.

Type B Warrior: Makes Decisions Based on the Faith of Others

TACTIC #2: ABORT

> Abort: "To terminate before completion."

Satan wants you to abort your faith, and he uses deception and doubt; deception about your relationship with God, and doubt about who God is and who you are. He wants you to abort your process of finding out who you are in Christ. He knows that if you were to ever find out who you really are, he would have hell to pay.

He wants you to abort the trials God is using to help build your faith. Remember, the trials presented to you are not to hurt or harm you, but to build your faith as you put total trust in God. Faith is the currency by which you communicate your needs to God, having total trust in His understanding and belief in His eternal purpose, plan, and will. Temptations arise from your old lifestyle, fight back by going deeper in the word and prayer in fasting. Stand firm in your identity as a child of God affirming your identity and your purpose daily. Your journey to self-discovery starts with you understanding the history between God and mankind. When you understand who you are as a child of God, your purpose will be revealed to you as you continue to seek aft er the knowledge of who God is. Remember God loves you and He sent Holy Spirit to do life with you to be your Comforter, your Guide, your Best Friend, and your Conscience.

> *"If you're afraid to fail, you'll be afraid to try.*
> *If you never try, you will never know your potential."*
> -Rumika McKnight

Defense:

- Have faith in God

- Know who you are

- Know your purpose

- Fast!

- Do not override the Holy Ghost convictions

- Persevere through your trials with God

- Do the Work. Obey!

Isaiah 41:10

Philippians 4:13

John 15:10-11

1 Thessalonians

5:16-18, Psalm 27

Prayer:

Heavenly Father, forgive me of my sins, and I forgive those who sinned against me. God, I want to please you in every way that I can, and I know this starts with me knowing who I am in You. Please put me on the path to discovering who You are. I know that when You reveal yourself to me, that I am made in Your image and likeness will find my identity in Christ Jesus. Lord, I just do not want to stop there, I want to discover and know my purpose. Your Word says that I am kept by Your power. Keep me in your word. Father I so dearly want to trust in You now that I know you have instilled your trust in me. Holy Spirit helps me to share my heart and mind with God acknowledging Him in all my ways.

Holy Spirit I desire to know you on a deeper level. My Father baptized me with Your Holy Spirit. Holy Spirit will you please make yourself known to me, and me more aware of Your presence. I can't do life without you. I don't want to do life without you. Be my comforter, helper, conscience, guide, and best friend. Most of all be Lord over my life. Father I know life will present me with some trying times internally and externally. Lord, wherever I lack self-love and have a poor self-image, bring healing to those areas of my life. Build my confidence, my heart, and mind in Your Word. Lord, when I am faced with a trial, help me to stick with it holding onto and trusting in You because I know that you are trying to build my faith. Lastly, help me to walk in obedience to you. I know that my faith is only operational when I do the works by obeying you. I ask all these things in the name of Jesus Christ my Lord and Savior.

Amen.

Section Six:

Stay Sober

TYPE C WARRIOR:

In your daily life, from the time you get up in the morning until the time yu lay down at night, you have a list of things running through your mind that you need to accomplish for that day. You may have multiple lists. You fill your mind with a mental to-do list, beginning with the needs of your family, spouse, chores around the house, to your job/career/school deadlines, bills and security, special projects, etc. Ask yourself, how much do I really get done, and how much of it spills over into the next day, then the next? Or if you do somehow manage to get it all done in one day, what state of mind are you in at the end of the day? Thrusting yourself in a never-ending cycle of familiarity called your daily routine. You wake up, follow steps 1,2,3, come home, shower, eat, go to sleep, and do it all again the next day. Either way, if you're not properly resting, you are tired, your brain is fried, your thoughts are scrambled, and you can hardly think straight.

When you are in that state of mind of constantly moving, and subconsciously doing without first checking or questioning your actions and environment, how coherent are you to make the proper decisions 1. daily? 2. Incident by incident? I knew Kamilah to be a prayer warrior; she was someone that I would constantly rely on for encouragement in my dark days. Because she was familiar with me, she allowed her guard to be let down, and before she knew it, the situation had escalated beyond her control.

TACTIC # 3 DECEPTION

Having a clear mind (head) in general is a very important tool in life. Much of what you experience on a day to day basis takes place in your mind. The way that you organize and engage in your thoughts affect the choices and the decisions that you make. It affects how you interact with those around you, it affects your perception of life, work, and family. It even affects your faith, your relationship with God the Father, the Son, and the Holy Spirit. It is important as a believer that you function with a clear mind. Outside of your natural responsibilities (home, work, social lives), you have a spiritual mandate in your life to be aware and knowledgeable about the tactics and devices [*2 Corinthians 2:11*] that Satan is using against you, your family, and those around you, to keep you in spiritual darkness. There must be a balance between your effectiveness and progress in the natural and spiritual.

1 Peter 5:8 admonishes,

Be sober, be vigilant; because YOUR adversary the devil walks about like a roaring lion, seeking whom he may devour. N.K.J.V.

There is a natural soberness that we as believers must maintain by abstaining from drugs and/or alcohol. To be sober in this manner is not to be under the influence or intoxicated by any foreign substance, alcohol, or narcotic and recreational drug. The basic biological fact is these substances affect the consciousness of an individual. When your consciousness is defective, the judgement in which you use to perceive situations and make sound rational decisions is inaccurate and erroneous. If you are an individual that uses alcohol or any type of drug, I cannot stress enough how detrimental this can be to your life and be a stumbling block in your relationship with God. Whether you are a heavy user, addict, or a functional user. If your desire is to really come to the true knowledge of God, make it an appoint to stop. Get help if you need to. Go to your Pastor, look for community resources, or ask a trusted friend to help you make the first step. Trust me when I say, the benefits from being free from that lifestyle are innumerable, and besides, you add time, vitality, and youth back to your life.

To be spiritually sober is to abstain from behaviors, thought patterns, and belief systems that can taint and influence your movement, judgement, decisions, and actions in the spiritual realm. Remember, we are engaging in a spiritual war that cannot be fought with physical weapons—therefore, the spiritual weapons that we do use (prayer, fasting, the Word, faith/trust) must be utilized with respect, responsibility, and reverence. Having a clear spiritual conscience is impertinent to ensuring that you are operating rightly and effectively in the spiritual realm.

Lest Satan should take advantage of us [you]; for we [you] are not ignorant of his devices.

2 Corinthians 2:11 N.K.J.V.

Here's a Truth: Satan hates you! THE DEVIL DOES NOT LIKE YOU! His objective against you and all believers in Christ is to kill you, steal from you, and destroy you, everything, and everybody connected to you: *John 10:10.* By now you should have the understanding that Satan is constantly working against all saints including you. 24 hours a day, 7 days a week, 52 weeks a year he is on the job with his satanic agents plotting, devising, scheming, setting traps to set you back or stagnate your growth in the spiritual principles are set forth in the Gospel and the Word of God. The Father is very concerned about you being a well- rounded individual and having a balanced life.

140

Beloved, I pray that you may prosper in all things and be in good health, just as your soul prospers.

3 John 1:2 N.K.J.V

A false balance is an abomination to the Lord.

Proverbs 11:1 K.J.V.

Who you are, and what God has called you to be carries great responsibilities in the natural? Whether you are a husband, wife, CEO, teacher, receptionist, student, work in the food service industry, whatever state you may find yourself in today, if you have confessed your belief in the life, death, and resurrection of Jesus Christ, you are first and foremost a child of God. Secondly, you have your responsibilities to fulfill as a husband, wife, CEO, or whatever God reveals your purpose to be.

I want you to understand two things about soberness: 1st: you can never let your natural responsibilities outweigh your spiritual responsibilities. You can never let what you do overshadow who you are. Your identity will always take precedence over your purpose. You are a child of God your purpose may be to be a loving husband or a lawyer. You are a child of God, but your purpose may be a wife, or doctor. You are a child of God, and your purpose may be to empower and encourage other individuals with your gift or talents. 2nd: You cannot be alert if you are not aware. You must first become aware of the dangers to yourself (physical), to your mind, to your heart, to your soul, and to your spirit to prepare and protect yourself for/from an attack. If you are not aware of the dangers, you will not know what to be on the lookout for.

Everything that you have, have accomplished, and have become, God has allowed you and given you the grace and favor to obtain these things. As you continue to seek Him, He will continue to reveal to you your purpose and the depth thereof.

Seek the Kingdom of God above all else and live righteously and He will give you everything you need.

Matthew 6:33 N.L.T.

It is very easy to get caught up in the cycles of everyday life. Obtaining the necessities of life is important to us all: financial security, shelter, food, and clothing. On top of that, we would like to be able to enjoy life recreationally: vacations, dinner at our favorite restaurant, catch a movie, or whatever it is you like to do leisurely or as a hobby. You want to be around the people you love, laugh until your belly hurts, and create great memories. The Father wants that for you too! What He does not want is for you to obtain everything you can from this world and forfeit your spot in eternity with Him Mark 8:36. For this, He warns us against our adversary and admonishes us to be sober and watchful.

SENSITIVITY AND DISCERNMENT

In the Christian community, you may or may not have heard the terms "Discernment" and "Sensitive to the Holy Spirit." Discernment and sensitivity are key and important to being and becoming aware, alert, and sober. Understanding discernment comes in two parts. There is the gift of discerning spirits and there is the spirit of discernment. The gift of the discerning of spirits is found in *1 Corinthians 10*.

There are diversities of gifts, but the same Spirit. There are differences between ministries, but the same Lord. And there are diversities of activities, but it is the same God who works all in all. But the manifestation of the Spirit is given to each one for the profit of all...to another the working of miracles, to another prophecy, to another discerning of spirits. But one and the same Spirit works all these things, distributing to each one individually as He wills.

1 Corinthians 12:4-6, 10-11 N.K.J.V.

Beloved, do not believe every spirit, but test the spirits, whether they are of God.

1 John 4:1 N.K.J.V.

So, the gift of discernment is a tool given to certain individuals, giving them the ability to spiritually see and pinpoint certain behaviors, patterns, and influences that manifests itself in people at a degree that is not spiritually given or obtained by others. Secondly, the spirit of discernment is given to all believers. Because you are a child of God you have His Spirit within you, the Holy Spirit. It is the Holy Spirit which helps you discern. Simply put, it is the ability to discern good from evil. The concept may be simply put, but the task is not. Remember a few chapters back in relating what God considers good, and what we consider good? Our goodness, or what we may call good is faulty because it is measured on the standard of our morals, desires, will, and intellect. Because of his Holiness, His goodness takes on a whole new meaning and dimension. For you to discern what is good and what is evil, you will have to get this standard and measuring tool from God through the Holy Spirit.

Which brings us to the topic of sensitivity.

Again, simply put, it is a believer's ability to sense or feel the leading of the Holy Spirit. The more time you spend with Him [in Word and Prayer], the more sensitive you will become to feeling his attendance and presence. Sensitivity and the spirit of discernment goes hand and hand. You cannot successfully navigate spiritual warfare having one without the other. Sensitivity tells you that something is there, discernment lets you know what it is. The danger in being spiritually sensitive without the Spirit of discernment is misdiagnosing and/or misjudging a situation or a person.

When you operate in the spirit of discernment alone you will be able to pinpoint what is right and wrong according to God's standards and His Word. Which is good, BUT what normally happens is when we see someone is good and bad, we judge that individual and/or their situation, making ourselves the judge and not God. The issue with only operating out of discernment is, you leave no room for mercy, grace, and love. Scripture says:

Do not judge, or you too will be judged. For in the same way, you judge others, you will be judged, and with the measure you use, it will be measured to you.

Matthew 7:1-2 N.I.V.

With the merciful God will show Himself merciful;
With a blameless man He will show Himself blameless.

Psalm 18:25 N.K.J.V.

Operating and functioning in sensitivity alone too has its dangers. When you became born again, God gave you His Holy Spirit. Receiving the Holy Spirit, by faith gave you an innate ability to feel [SENSE] another dimension, the spiritual world. Having been exposed to the spiritual world, you cannot be naïve to think that you will only feel [sense] only the "good things", mainly the Holy Spirit. The spiritual realm is much like the natural realm in that it has both elements, good and evil. The reason that you have become sensitive to the demonic realm is because Satan has picked you up on his radar, as a child of God. Since you are new to this, he uses this as an opportunity to infiltrate himself into your life, bringing confusion with the purpose of leading you astray. If you are functioning on sensitivity alone without discernment, you will make the mistake of thinking you are being led by the Holy Spirit, and it will reveal it to be the total opposite. Sensitivity by being born again in Christ, exposes you not just to the Holy Spirit, but to the whole spiritual dimensions.

But if the Spirit of Him who raised Jesus from the dead dwell in you, He that raised up Christ from the dead shall also quicken [Legal access to the spiritual realm] your mortal bodies by His Spirit who dwelleth in you [guides you].

Romans 8:11 K.J.V.

Discernment enables you to tell whether it's good [God/ the Holy Spirit] or bad [Satan/ his forces of darkness]. You need to be sensitive to the Holy Spirit as well have His discernment, so you do not make the mistakes of wrongly judging or being led away by a

145

spirit that is not of God. Tapping into the spiritual realm illegally, without the Holy Ghost, will cause you to fall into the practices of witchcraft. God frowns upon witchcraft. He detests it, and it is NOT His will for your life.

Be sober, be vigilant, because the enemy, your adversary the devil, walketh about seeking whom he may devour. 1 Peter 5:8

All of these principles make up a sober mind: awareness, alertness, sensitivity, and discernment. Being sober minded is a choice, a decision. It's an intentional choice and decision daily and regularly, with the understanding of what's at stake. I don't want to sound all doom and gloom, but with all seriousness, your life, your soul is at stake. Even the life of those you lead (family), or those who look up to you and will count on you for spiritual guidance. Not only does your life depend on it, but to some degree others' lives as well. I will say this again,

SATAN DOES NOT LIKE YOU AT ALL! He does not like what you stand for, he doesn't care about your family, and he strongly hates that you have a relationship with God and are welcomed in His Presence.

The definition of hate is to feel INTENSE or passionate DISLIKE for someone. The truth is Satan covets what you have. There is nothing like wanting something that is always and forever beyond your reach. That "thing" is salvation. Satan can never receive salvation. He has already been judged.

Satan, who is the god of this world.

2 Corinthians 4:4 N.L.T

Judgment will come because the ruler of this world has already been judged.

John 16:11 N.L.T.

Then the devil, who had deceived them, was thrown into the fiery lake of burning sulfur, joining the beast and the false prophet. There they will be tormented day and night forever and ever.

Revelation 20:10 N.L.T.

Satan is well aware of his final resting place! He will be thrown into the lake of fire along with death and hell, and that's where he and those deceived by him will spend the rest of eternity. He knows this! And because he knows this, he wants to take as many people with him as possible, and he does this through deception. Satan's deception works like this: he'll give you 10% truth, but the other 90% is a lie. At the sum of it, the whole idea, thought, or statement may seem like the truth or the will of God because of the truth that was presented in it, but as you dig deeper, you will discover the truth was a mask for his lies and deception.

> Deceive [verb]: "(of a person) cause (someone) to believe something that is not true, typically in order to gain some personal advantage."

This brings me back to the central scripture of this chapter: Be sober, be vigilant; because YOUR adversary the devil walks about like a roaring lion, seeking whom he may devour. To devour, in its original context means to drink down; to engulf wholly, with the purpose of getting drunk. Satan wants to destroy every single part of you, everything that you are connected to, and all that are connected to you. Satan is intoxicated with the blood of men, and he relishes in the moment when he can lead one of us away from the Kingdom. His drunkenness is never satisfied, he wants more. He wants you!

I just Don't Get it?

Lest Satan should take advantage of us; for we are not ignorant of his devices.

2 Corinthians 2:11 N.K.J.V.

Remember in Tactic #1 Sabotage. He wants to sabotage your relationship with God. Tactic #2 he wants you to abort your faith and your assignments. His ultimate goal is and will always be to lead you away from God. I am going to be completely honest with you, there is no clear steps that myself or anyone can give you in spotting out the deceptive devices of the Satan, but you have an Advocate, Helper, Teacher, Counselor, and Friend given to you by the Father, entrusted with your care, and Satan is no match for Him! Remember Kamilah's story. We were good friends, used to being around one another, so to her there was no need for her to have her guard up or remain sober minded around me. To her there was no reason for her to be alert or remain aware in her environment. This is the danger I want to warn you about and press upon you the need to be alert, aware, sensitive, and discerning at all times and towards everyone. To reiterate:

> Sober Mindedness = Alertness + Awareness + Discernment + Sensitivity

It is a conscious choice, and a daily practice that you should put into play. The more you make this your aim and focus, the stronger your spiritual radar will become. This is not something that you receive, gain, or go aft er in your own strength, but by making the Lord aware of this desire of your heart in prayer, the Holy Spirit coaches you by bringing these things to your remembrance and speaking to your God conscience, as long as you do the work of feeding your spirit the Word of God, and living a lifestyle of consistent fasting and prayer.

Kamilah said in the interview, "Something triggered in my spirit, but I did not adhere to it because it was you. Rumika, my friend." That something was someone, the Holy Ghost. Kamilah failed to, at that moment, adhere to the leadership of the Holy Spirit, who was trying to warn her that something was wrong! To be spiritually sober is to be free from behaviors, thought patterns, and belief systems that can taint and influence your movement, judgement, decisions, and actions. Spiritual soberness is a tool that is given to you for you to be able to detect that something is wrong, what it is, and what to do. Do not override the Holy Spirit when He is setting off triggers in you that something is wrong? Take a step back, silence your thoughts, and take a different look at the situation, person, idea, with the help of the Holy Spirit. He is alerting and warning you, that if you continue to proceed you will fall prey to the deception of Satan and he will take advantage of you.

My experience and example with Kamilah were intense, and in some cases extreme, but the Lord did intervene. If anything, I believe that this experience served as a wake-up call to her. The enemy's tactics and devices come in many different forms and ways. He usually tempts us with things we love, hold dear to us, or sentimentally connected to. Because these things are wrapped in our emotions, we sometimes look past the fact that any danger or harm can be connected to these things or people. The more you operate from an alert, aware, discerning, and sensitive place, the more sober minded you will be in the face of danger and avoid it as best as you can with the help of the Holy Spirit.

Being sober-minded is a strength and a great tool to have in your belt. It's one of those tools that bears fruit in your life, as well as empower you to cover [pray for] others who may need help, be in danger, or going down the wrong path. Sometimes it's not easy approaching people with what the Lord shows you in the Spirit, you don't have to approach them, but you can always pray for them.

The earnest prayer of a righteous person has great power and produces wonderful results.

James 5:16 N.L.T.

Type C Warrior: Has Their Guard Down
TACTIC #3 DECEPTION

Deceive: To mislead by false appearance or statement

Satan wants to destroy you by deceiving you and taking advantage of you. Th e truth is he hates you and covets your relationship with God. He is never satisfied from the blood of men fallen prey to his devices, he will continually come aft er you. Build your best relationship with the Holy Spirit. He is your first defense. Build up your sensitivity and discernment by becoming sharp in the Word of God. Have a consistent lifestyle of prayer and fasting. All of these helps you to remain alert and aware, so when the Holy Spirit intervenes you can listen intently as he reveals and gives you instructions.

Defense:

- BE alert
- BE aware
- DISCERN all things
- Stay SENSITIVE to the Holy Spirit by daily growing in your relationship with Him. In the Word, prayer, and fasting

1 Thessalonians 5:6-10

1 John 4:1

John 14: 15-18

Hosea 14:9

Philippians 1:9-10

I just Don't Get it?

Let us pray:

Father God, I repent daily of my sins before you. Please help me to always walk in forgiveness towards all who may have offended me or hurt me. Father I know that being sober minded is important to you, because it helps protect me and those connected to me from being deceived and taken advantage of by Satan. I ask today that you make this a desire of my heart.

Teach me what it is to be alert, aware, discerning, and sensitive. Help me grow in my relationship with the Holy Spirit by staying consistent in prayer, studying and reading the Word, and fasting. Increase my hunger and desire to do these things. Holy Spirit you have my permission to hold me accountable. Father helped me to recognize the triggers of the Holy Spirit so that I may adhere to them, and not override them. As I grow, put others in my path so that I may cover them in prayer, knowing that you will hear me and intervene on their behalf.

In Jesus Name, Amen.

MY TRUTH

The Truth is short, sweet, and simple and within it lies layers. The Truth is about discovery. I discovered so much about myself on this journey, so much about God. I discovered the confidence and the love which lie on the inside of me, to know and understand myself truly and be ok with-it all.

Finding out the Truth in Christ is the best thing that has ever happened to me. It has redefined my perception of culture, relationships, and purpose. I cannot pinpoint where I was before emotionally, mentally, spiritually. I was like you and most people, doing the best I could to get by. Having fun here and there living what I thought at the time was my best life, or just nonchalantly skating through life. It wasn't until my life came to hard place that I started to think Nd feel "there has to be more to life than this. If there is a God, where is He because I need Him to make it all make sense.".

I found myself confused, lost, ashamed. Confused wondering "How did I end up here?". Lost because I did not know "where" I was. What was my life about up to this point, and what will it be like tomorrow, the next day, and the next? Ashamed because I felt like I owed myself, others, the world more than I had given up to this point. But Holy Ghost would not allow me to settle where I was emotionally in the dumps, spiritually dead, and mentally discombobulated. So, I decided to seek and follow through with Truth.

See that is the thing. We can seek after or discover a thing, but then throw it away once we satisfied our high or experienced the adrenaline of the chase. You cannot do that with God. You cannot do that with Truth. This Truth is hard because it holds mirror to

153

the real you surpassing the superficiality of what you put on display for the world to see. This Truth breaks every molecule apart, and as hard as you my try, you cannot hide from it. If you're not humble in your pursuit, it'll make your transition more challenging. This Truth my seem damaging maybe even hurtful, but its power is to heal, restore, reconcile. Looking back over my life all I ever wanted was love and truth. God knew that about me. He understood that about me, and He obliged by sharing his life's story with me and revealing His place in mine. God took me on this journey. He was spontaneous, humorous, structured, patient, kind, loving, mind blowing helping me self-evolve. I found myself in love again, alive again.

The worldly things that I desired would no longer hold a candle to the life I am living now. I have found peace and purpose! Aw man, there is so much I can say, but these will be things that I realized and discovered on my own journey. This is my story, my faith. You have this same opportunity to discover, evolve, reconcile, be whole, and complete. You have to make the same decisions I did and go for God in Spirit and in Truth. God has blessed me to give unto you so many keys to the Kingdom to shift your mindset and your way of thinking. Reread them, study them, use them!

God is so real and tangible to me, so my heart is to make Him known in any way I can to whomever I can. I desire to be like Him: holy, loving, and pure in every way. My heart's desire is for you to KNOW Jesus.

There is a lot of doctrine floating around that has a form of godliness, but there is nothing like picking the fruit off the tree yourself. I pray this book has been a blessing to you, your family, and those you share it with. Now, what is your truth? And what are you going to do about it?

I would love to hear from you. If this series has been a blessing to your life or ministry, please write me:

soulsalvationbook@gmail.com

Made in the USA
Columbia, SC
28 July 2021